CW01335725

A Medieval
Cornish Miscellany

A Medieval
Cornish Miscellany

W. M. M. Picken

edited by O. J. Padel

Phillimore

2000

Published by
PHILLIMORE & CO. LTD.
Shopwyke Manor Barn, Chichester, West Sussex

© W. M. M. Picken, 2000

ISBN 1 86077 098 3

Printed and bound in Great Britain by
THE CROMWELL PRESS

Contents
(with places of previous publication)

Editor's Preface .... *vii*
Abbreviations .... *viii*

1 **The Landochou Charter** *1*
W. G. Hoskins, *The Westward Expansion of Wessex* (Leicester, 1960), 36-44

2 **The Manor of Tremaruustel and the Honour of St Keus** *12*
Journal of the Royal Institution of Cornwall, n.s., 7 (1973-7), 220-30

3 **Bishop Wulfsige Comoere: an unrecognised 10th-century gloss in the Bodmin Gospels** *28*
Cornish Studies, 14 (1986), 34-8

4 **Tremail and Turgoil in Domesday Book** *34*
Devon and Cornwall Notes and Queries, 36 (1987-91), 269-73

5 **Cornish Place-Names and Fiefs in a 12th-Century Charter** *39*
Cornish Studies, 13 (1985), 55-61

6 **Trezance, Lahays and the Manor of Cardinham** *50*
Devon and Cornwall Notes and Queries, 26 (1954-5), 203-8

7 **A Misdated Cornish Tax Account in the Book of Fees** *58*
Cornish Studies, 10 (1982), 19-25

8 **Light on Lammana** *69*
Devon and Cornwall Notes and Queries, 35 (1982-6), 281-6

9   **The Names of the Hundreds of Cornwall** *76*
    Devon and Cornwall Notes and Queries, 30 (1965-7), 36-40

10 **The Earliest Borough Charter of East Looe** *81*
    Journal of the Royal Institution of Cornwall, n.s., 8 (1978-81), 350-7

11 **The Descent of Willington from Robert, Earl of Gloucester** ... *92*
    Not previously published

12 **The Patron Saints of Poundstock and Helland Churches** *113*
    Devon and Cornwall Notes and Queries, 23 (1947-9), 342-3

13 **St German of Cornwall's Day** *115*
    Devon and Cornwall Notes and Queries, 27 (1956-8), 103-7

14 **Callington and Kelliwic** *121*
    Devon and Cornwall Notes and Queries, 27 (1956-8), 225-7

15 **The Feudality of Pendrim Manor** *125*
    Not previously published

    Publications of W. M. M. Picken *135*

Editor's Preface

Martin Picken was born in the rectory, St Martin by Looe, Cornwall, in December 1906. He read history at Sidney Sussex College, Cambridge, and then for the ministry at Westcott House, Cambridge. After a short spell in Yorkshire he returned to Cornwall, and in 1937, after his father's death, to St Martin's as rector himself. In 1971 he retired to Falmouth, where he died in November 1998, a month before his 92nd birthday. His ashes were buried at St Martin's on Martinmas 1998.

During his time in Cornwall he built on the scholarly work which Charles Henderson had begun, collecting forms for Cornish place-names with a view to elucidating both the names themselves and the history of the places to which they refer. To that end he took a particular interest in family history and manorial descent, realising that these branches of history are essential for the accurate identification of place-name forms found in early records. The types of record in which he took a particularly close interest were inquisitions post mortem and manorial rentals and surveys.

Before his death he suggested to me, as his literary executor, that some of his publications (of which a full list appears below) could usefully be collected together and reprinted. I wholeheartedly agreed, and have added two essays which he left unpublished. The first ('The descent of Willington') had received his final adjustments for publication; but the second ('The feudality of Pendrim') had not yet satisfied his demanding standards. It is included here with diffidence, but in the belief that the suggestion, with accompanying discussion, is worth publishing for the consideration of others, whether or not it will be vindicated by later work.

Since some of the essays appeared some time ago (one as much as 50 years), I have inserted a few references to more recent work where it seemed advisable. These take the form of notes in square brackets at the ends of the chapters. I have also corrected a few very minor misprints or other errors, and occasionally updated references, where documents referred to in manuscript have subsequently been published. But complete consistency in the references has not been attempted. Much of what I have been able to add in the way of expansion or, occasionally, correction is due to the author's generous and patient teaching concerning Cornish history and its documentation, particularly in the field of manorial history, over many years. It is right that the fruits of his learning, from which I have benefited so greatly, should be shared as widely as possible.

Thanks are gladly given to the editors of the journals where these essays first appeared, for permission to reprint them, and to others who have assisted in the preparation of the volume for the press, particularly chapters 11 and 15: Dr. Nicholas Vincent, Dr. Brian Golding, Mr. Keith Hamylton Jones, Dr. Robert Bearman, Dr. Joanna Mattingly, Mr. John Southern and Mr. David Thomas.

O.J.P.

Abbreviations

Anc.D	*Catalogue of Ancient Deeds*, Vol. IV (H.M.S.O., 1902)
CRO	Cornwall County Record Office, Truro
CSS	*Cornish Saints Series*; booklets by G. H. Doble, 1923-45
DB	*Domesday Book seu Liber Censualis* (Record Commissioners, 1783-1816): four volumes of which I and II contain the *Exchequer Domesday* and IV contains the *Exeter Domesday*
DCRS	Devon & Cornwall Record Society publication
DRO	Devon County Record Office, Exeter
Exon.DB	The Exeter Domesday Book in DB IV (Record Commissioners, 1816)
Hingeston-Randolph	F. C. Hingeston-Randolph, *Episcopal Registers of the Diocese of Exeter*; the volume is indicated by the bishop's name
Launceston Cartulary	*The Cartulary of Launceston Priory (Lambeth Palace MS. 719). A Calendar*, edited by P. L. Hull, DCRS, n.s., 30 (1987)
LL	*Liber Landavensis*: The Book of Llan Dâv (ed. J.G. Evans), Oxford, 1893
Mon.Angl.	W. Dugdale, *Monasticon Anglicanum* (London, 1818-20)
Mon.Exon.	G. Oliver, *Monasticon Dioecesis Exoniensis* (Exeter, 1846)
PRO	MS. in Public Record Office (London)
PRS	Pipe Roll Society publications
RC	Record Commissioners' publication
RIC	MS. in Royal Institution of Cornwall (Truro)
SC	*The Saints of Cornwall*; reprints (6 vols., 1960-97) of parts of Doble's CSS
TM	Sir John Maclean, *History of the Deanery of Trigg Minor*, 3 vols. (London etc., 1873-9)
T.Reg	Transcript, in C. G. Henderson's calendar 23, of the register (destroyed by enemy action in 1942) of Trelawny muniments compiled in 1598

1
The 'Landochou' Charter

W. G. Hoskins, *The Westward Expansion of Wessex* (Leicester, 1960), 36-44.

AMONG THE CHANCERY MISCELLANEA in the Public Record Office at London there lies, unaccountably ignored, a manuscript purporting to be a copy of one of King Edgar's charters. It concerns the minster that has since become the parish church of St Kew in north Cornwall, near the site of an ancient Celtic monastery. In King Edgar's day the monastery was called *Landochou,* from which name (in later forms such as Lanow) the usurping secular manor there, and for a time the parish and the parish church, all took their title.

The manuscript is one of three relating to a certain prior of Plympton's petition to the king-in-council against a judgement delivered at Launceston during the Cornish eyre of 1302 touching this church of Lanow *alias* St Kew.[1] The first of the three, which are all filed together, is this copy of King Edgar's charter;[2] the second is a copy of a writ of *Certiorari super recordo,* dated 27 October in the year 1305 and addressed to the chief justice of that eyre; and the third is a copy of his undated return to this writ, reciting the required record of the Launceston judgement. It may be remarked that the handwriting of the charter appears to be identical with that of one of the compilers of the *Rex* roll of the same Launceston assize.[3] All three manuscripts therefore, and in particular that of the charter, may be assigned to the period *c.*1305. It is even possible to trace the prescript calling them into being, for when the prior presented his appeal an order was made that a writ of *Certiorari super recordo* touching his judgement be sent to the chief justice of the Cornish eyre, that the charters and the process be examined, and that any necessary consequent action be taken.[4] These three documents in the Record Office

---
[1] For the text of the petition see Maclean, *History of Trigg Minor*, II, 1887, p. 270.
[2] C47/52/1/1, m. 3.
[3] PRO, Just.1/117.
[4] Maclean, *loc. cit.* (Responsio).

must be survivors of the little collection of evidences gathered together under that order.

Judging by its contents the charter was put in evidence by the prior himself, for it does not say what, according to his opponents, it ought to have said. Its silence on certain issues vaguely supported the prior's case: unfortunately there is reason to think that its text had already been censored in the prior's interest. The case of the Cornishmen against the prior at the assize of 1302 was one of neglect of duty at Lanow church. They asserted that King Edgar had given Lanow church with two carucates of land and a hundred shillings' rent to 'canons of Plympton' for the purpose of supporting two of them in perpetual residence at Lanow in order to offer hospitality, distribute alms, and celebrate divine service for the souls of the donor and his successors; and they further asserted that the prior of Plympton, who (they said) was now responsible for maintaining these services at Lanow, had withdrawn his two canons-regular, and with them the performance of these services, from Lanow for the past 15 years. The prior defended the charge. He produced in court the charter whereby William Warelwast, Bishop of Exeter, recorded his unconditional gift of Lanow church to Plympton Priory; he also produced the charter of King Henry II confirming this bishop's gift. The prior's facts were perfectly correct. Warelwast and his cathedral church at Exeter had been given Lanow church by King Henry I by a charter datable to the year 1123;[5] soon afterwards the bishop seems to have transferred the Cornish church to his newly founded priory at Plympton. The text of his charter doing this no longer survives, but it was known to Bishop Walter Bronescombe of Exeter in 1261,[6] and was, as already stated, produced in court in 1302. The text of the royal confirmation does survive, and substantiates the prior's statement.[7] In spite of these circumstances the prior lost the verdict at the assize court and was ordered to restore two resident canons to Lanow to perform the specified duties. When the prior petitioned the king against this decision he got little satisfaction. The judgement of 1302 was reiterated, with the sole

[5] J. H. Round, *Feudal England*, pp. 482 sqq., discusses the date of this charter, which is printed by Dugdale, *Mon. Angl.*, VI, p. 53, and by Oliver, *Monasticon Dioecesis Exoniensis* (Exeter, 1846), p. 134. The MS. has 'Tohou' for Dohou.
[6] F. C. Hingeston-Randolph, *The Registers of Walter Bronescombe and Peter Quivel* (London & Exeter, 1889), p. 224.
[7] Oliver, *op. cit.*, p. 135, no. III (from Charter Roll, 22 July 1328).

concession that two resident secular clergy might be substituted at Lanow for the two regular ones.[8]

Now these judgements are of practical importance to us in assessing the value of the charter. They can only be based on the conviction that in its relevant particulars the Cornish tradition about King Edgar's reorganisation at Lanow church spoke true, and that the terms of his donation bound all who subsequently came to hold his gift, howsoever acquired. These judgements clothe the Cornish traditional account of King Edgar's acts with very considerable authority, so that it can be used as a check upon the veracity of the charter. The tradition comes well accredited; but the charter comes as an *ex parte* document from Plympton priory (the transcriber himself wrote the word *Plumpton* on the foot of this copy) produced by those who stood to gain or lose most heavily from what it said.

The text is clearly written on well-preserved but not quite rectangular parchment, 7 13/16 in. wide by 3 3/16 in. high at the centre. Except for the heading and the subscribed word *Plumpton* the writing runs from margin to margin, without formal spacing like that now added in this publication (where oblique lines indicate line-endings in the manuscript).

CARTA REGIS EDGARI[9]

✠ In nomine domini nostri Jhesu Christi . Omnia vero inuisibilia que corporalibus nostris obtutibus clancula atque absconsa sunt . et terrena[10]/ ac inmutabilia existunt . Qui igitur tunc istic[11] pregrauatis humanisque visionibus temporaliter patent caduca et transitoria/ [i]ustisima ratione deputentur. Qua propter ego Eadgar diuina dispensacione Rex . Ongilsaxonum[12] partes aliquas terre . Hoc est mensu/ra duarum Mans[a]rum[13] in Monasterio quod ab incolis Landochou vocitatur . istis duobus sanctis Dochou et Cypa[14] pro dei amore in

---

[8] *Calendar of Patent Rolls, 1301-7*, p. 512.

[9] In the MS. this heading is not all in capital letters.

[10] Something is wrong. Dr. Finberg plausibly suggests that *et terrena* started as *eterna*.

[11] *Sic*; the original reading was perhaps 'Que igitur tunc istis …'.

[12] The style *rex* or *basileus Angul Saxonum* is common in Eadwig's charters, but very rare in Edgar's; it does however occur in W. de G. Birch, *Cartularium Saxonicum*, 3 vols. (London, 1885-93), III, no. 1183.

[13] In the traditional account these two hides become two carucates.

[14] In Cornwall the name of St Docco eventually became Dawe. For *Cypa* read Cywa. A *wyn* has been mistaken for the letter 'p'. The name originated as Caio, according to J. Loth, *Les Noms des Saints Bretons* (Paris, 1910). Later it became Cyw, and was latinised as Cywa. The final Cornish form was Kew.

eternam/ hereditatem largitus sum cum omnibus ad se rite pertinentibus . campis, siluis, pascuis, Riuolis, fluminibus, pratis . Ea condicione[15]/ ut habeant eam terram liberam sine fine precipiendo precipio . In nomine omnipotentis dei ut ad Monasterium Sancti Dochou et Sancte Cypa pre/fata terra reddatur ubi reliquie eorum piissimorum patroniorum honorifice obseruantur . Hec sunt nomina consenciencium huic regali/donacioni .

✠ . Eadgar Rex signo sancte crucis meam Munificenciam conroboraui .
✠ . Ego Daniel Episcopus[16] consensi et subscripsi/
✠ . Ego Aelfþolt Episcopus[17] consensi et subscripsi .
✠ . Ego Osþolt Episcopus[18] consensi subscripsi
✠ . Ego Aelfre[19] Dux consensi .
✠ . Ego Aeþstan[20]/Dux consensi .
✠ . Ego Aeþelþolt[21] Dux consensi

Hec sunt territoria istius agelluli primitus a pont Magano[22] in Longitudine Riuo/lis usque ad þuern golornan[23] deinde ad pentalou[24] usque per siluam de Penfynfos . deinde ad fynnian iacu[25] . deinde usque penma/yn Cenþuerehit nahal[26] de poll duu[27] . iterum de pont Magano . Hic est terminus prefati Agelluli quisquis hoc

---

[15] *Ea condicione* seems to me abrupt and anachronistic, though the phrase is found also in the rather corrupt charter of King Athelstan to St Buryan Church in Cornwall (Birch, *Cartularium Saxonicum*, II, no. 785). There are marked similarities of form and diction between these two charters. In this case I suggest that the phrase was inserted as a stop-gap to mask an omission.

[16] Daniel, Bishop of Cornwall, as *chorepiscopus* of the Bishop of Crediton (see n. 35), signing 955-9.

[17] Ælfwold, Bishop of Crediton, signing 953-70; or Ælfwold, Bishop of Sherborne, signing 961-75. [The 14th-century scribe's representation of Anglo-Saxon *wynn*, serving in this and the following names for both *wynn* and *thorn*, has here been reproduced with þ. O.J.P.]

[18] Oswald, Bishop of Worcester, consecrated 961.

[19] Ælfhere.

[20] Æthelstan.

[21] Æthelwold.

[22] The substance of the notes on this and the following Old-Cornish words was kindly communicated to me by the late R. Morton Nance in a letter dated 27 November 1957. *Pont* is a Cornish word, and *Magano* might represent the personal name Matganoe, 'wellborn', meaning 'Magano's bridge'.

[23] *Wuern golornan* or *golornau*. Gwern, 'marsh', followed by an unknown word.

[24] *Pentalou*. Pen tal lon might be 'top' or 'end of the brow of the grove'.

[25] *Fynnian iacu*. Fynyow (*fynniau*) Iacu, 'Jago's boundaries'. (A field in St Kew parish called Yago in 1841 must have been fairly near the old boundary between Lanow Mur and Lanow Saint manors; nevertheless it is difficult to believe the resemblance between the ancient and the modern names is not fortuitous.—W.M.M.P.)

[26] *Penmayn Cenwuerehit nahal*. Pen men, 'stone end' or 'top'. The rest is unintelligible. R.M.N. noticed *kenwerthek*, 'market place', but thought it an unlikely identification. Also doubtful is *uahal* for gwal, 'wall'.

[27] *Poll duu*. Pol duu, 'black pool', or pol dun, 'deep pool'.

fregerit hoc nostrum donum sciat[28] se anathematizatum esse coram deo . Amen ∴.

Plumpton

As it stands the text cannot be a *bona fide* copy, even an inferior one, of a complete charter of King Edgar. There are omissions and obscurities, which will be discussed in due course, proving as much beyond doubt. Yet it does not read like a thoroughgoing forgery: it has an oddly disjointed style for one thing, and for another it is far too pointless. Moreover, though the form looks dislocated, most of the language looks genuine. But the really decisive evidence that it is much more than mere fiction comes from the text itself: it contains three features that no Anglo-Norman forger after the Conquest could have invented. They prove that part at least of the text, if not the whole, derives from some genuine 10th-century charter about *Landochou*.

First, there is the spelling of the place-name *Landochou*[29] and of the allied personal name *Dochou*. These forms had become archaic in Cornwall by 1086. Though *Landochou* is instanced as a spelling of Welsh versions of the same name (cf. two places now called Llandough in Glamorgan, and Llandogo in Monmouthshire) it is found as a spelling of the Cornish place-name only in this example. At the date of Domesday Book the sound 'ch' in Cornish speech from being an explosive had become a spirant, commonly written as 'h'. This place-name is mentioned five times altogether in Domesday Book and the Exeter Domesday in connection with the Cornish manor there (the church is unnoticed), and though the scribes never got it quite right—*Lannohoo* and *Lantloho*, for instance—their misspellings do not conceal the fact that the version aimed at was *Landohou* or *Landoho*, not *Landochou*.[30] And indeed *Landoho* remained the standard spelling for the next 100 years. So also with the personal name here written *Dochou*—correctly, for a mid-10th-century spelling: it suffered the same kind of change and is not found so spelt in any other surviving record of Cornish provenance. On the next mention of the church, in the

---

[28] *Sciat* is a contemporary interlineation scrawled by another hand over a deleted word that looks like *sciad*.
[29] Originally Lan-docco, 'monastic enclosure of Docco'. This Cornish monastery of St Docco, or Dawe, is mentioned in the oldest *Vita Samsonis*, written perhaps as early as the seventh century.
[30] DB I, p. 120; IV, pp. 92, 217, 470, 471.

charter of 1123, this saint's name, too, was written with 'h' instead of 'ch'.

The second textual feature referred to is the information that at the date of this charter there was a *monasterium* at which St Dawe and St Kew (Dochou and Cywa) were honoured as *joint* patrons and where their bodies rested—for that is the import of the remark about their relics. This joint patronage and the burials, by the way, have been unknown to students, though it was evident that the two cults had overlapped. Now there is reason to think, from a passage in the Exeter Domesday, that St Kew's cult at this *monasterium*, this minster [of Lanow], became the predominant one some considerable time before the Norman Conquest, largely ousting that of St Dawe. There is further evidence of this in the early 12th century, when the contemporary Martyrology of Exeter Cathedral (to which Lanow church then briefly belonged) made no mention of St Dawe on his day (15 February), though it duly entered St Kew's name on hers.[31] This charter reflects an earlier state of affairs at Lanow church than that of the 12th century, and probably than that of the 11th: St Dawe and St Kew appear in a more primitive and coequal fashion.

The third feature is the list of witnesses—a matter (it may for once be truthfully and literally said) of crucial importance. Debased by copyists' blunders though their names may be, they are nevertheless those of people who all could (and in probably two instances people who by virtue of their office *should*) have witnessed such a charter as this in the year 961, or less probably 962. The *terminus a quo* for dating this witness-list is the consecration in 961 of Bishop Oswald [of Worcester], one of the witnesses: the *terminus ad quem* is the date in 963 of the earliest known signature of Bishop Wulfsige of Cornwall,[32] whose predecessor, Bishop Daniel, is another witness. It has been shown elsewhere that Daniel was alive in October 959, not improbably dying on the 8th October 961; and that Wulfsige was the next Cornish bishop.[33] In any case the year 962 is the latest to which Daniel's episcopate can reasonably be stretched, since Wulfsige was in office in 963. It was fitting that the two west-country bishops, Ælfwold [of Crediton][34] and Daniel, his *chorepiscopus*

---

[31] 8 February.—Dean and Chapter of Exeter MS. 3518, ff. 1ᵛ, 1ʳ. This MS. is analysed by G. H. Doble in *Ordinale Exon.*, IV (Henry Bradshaw Soc., vol. LXXIX).

[32] Birch, *Cartularium Saxonicum*, III, no. 1118.

[33] See chapter 3. William of Malmesbury's impossible date DCCCCLVI for Bishop Daniel's death is probably DCCCCLXI miscopied.

[34] He attests 953-70. Or, less appropriately, Ælfwold of Sherborne, attesting 961-75.

The 'Landochou' Charter

[of Cornwall], should have witnessed this charter about establishments within their jurisdictions.[35] Apart from King Edgar himself the lay witnesses are Ælfhere, *dux*, Æthelstan, *dux*, and Æthelwold, *dux*: these men signed together a number of charters in the years 961 and 962, but after that Æthelwold attested very few.[36]

On the discredit side of the ledger must first of all be set the omissions and obscurities of the text that have already been mentioned. Vocabulary and syntax on the whole will pass muster: it is the tenor of the contents that is less than satisfactory. The Grant section, most important of all, is the worst offender. Here we look for details about the donor, about the donation, about the beneficiaries, and about the conditions of the transaction; but we find little indeed about the last two items. The donor is King Edgar; the donation is of two hides of land said, rather cryptically, to be *in* the monastery (*in Monasterio*) called *Landochou*. But as to beneficiaries, though St Dawe and St Kew are indeed named as such, the real ones, that is to say the human beings who would receive this donation, are never mentioned at all. Nor is it at first explained where and what the establishment of these two saints might be: only in a later rather clumsily introduced qualifying clause is the establishment casually revealed to be the minster (*Monasterium*) of the saints where they were venerated and buried. Without some knowledge of Lanow's long history we should have difficulty in recognising from this obscure account that the first *monasterium* where the land lay was the ancient and important, but presumably recently suppressed, Celtic monastery of Landochou, standing on or near the site of the present farmhouse called Lanow; and that the second, the *monasterium* of St Dawe and St Kew, was the minster standing where St Kew's Church now stands—the church that was to bring so much litigation upon the priors of Plympton. It is distant half a mile from Lanow, though it formerly took its name from the encircling manor that sprang from that place.[37] Clearly,

---

[35] Dr. Finberg has shown that the Cornish bishops of this period were *chorepiscopi* under the bishops of Crediton.—*Trans. Royal Hist. Soc.*, 5th ser., III, 1953, pp. 115-20.

[36] Twice more: Birch, *Cartularium Saxonicum*, III, nos. 1103 (dated 963) and 1135 (964); but on this last cf. E. John, *Land Tenure in Early England* (Leicester, 1960), p. 98.

[37] Lanow became the capital of the important secular manor called at different times Landoho, Lanou, or Lanow Mur ('Great Lanow'). The church borrowed these names, though not the adjective Mur. It was also sometimes called the church of Lanow Saint—the name of its glebe (from *Lanou sant*, 'Holy Lanow').

some vital particulars have dropped out of this section. And not only particulars about the beneficiaries, but about the conditions of the donation, too. In spite of the phrase 'ea condicione' no real conditions are given at all in the charter, not even the almost inevitable *trinoda necessitas*. These are the gravest omissions and obscurities: they cannot but be deliberate. Fortunately Cornish tradition enables most of these losses to be supplied: the beneficiaries at the minster were the canons of Plympton, in Devonshire; the conditions of the donation were those which the priors of Plympton were accused in 1302 of neglecting. Naturally enough no tradition about the *trinoda necessitas* survived: there was no reason to remember it. There may be other omissions—a Dating section perhaps, and possibly a Sanction (the short sentence at the end hardly seems adequate). Certain further faults are less damaging to the probity of the text, such as the distorted spellings of some personal names, which can perhaps be dismissed as the well-meant or accidental contributions of copyists. The punctuation, not surprisingly, is erratic; but at least it proves a degree of antiquity in the charter. The text must necessarily be older than the manuscript so punctuated.

There is a Survey of the boundary, very brief, but including some interesting Old-Cornish words. For comment upon these I am indebted to the late R. Morton Nance. The text here is not free from the suspicion of miscopying and in one passage is unintelligible. For this or some other reason these boundaries have not yet been identified with places in St Kew parish or its vicinity. They may refer to the old rectorial glebe of Lanow church which the Austin canons of Plympton called their manor of Lanow Saint, 'Holy Lanow'. But that manor was dismembered and sold after the Dissolution, and its early boundaries are not very exactly known. Finally, it is apparent that the transcriber of this text, or of an earlier recension of it, was working from a manuscript in which Anglo-Saxon *thorns* and *wyns* were employed—to his confusion. He transcribed them all, indiscriminately, as *wyns*; and some of the witnesses' names suffered in consequence. Of the same category of error is his rendering of the saint's name Cywa as *Cypa*—an absurd blunder, but showing that the name stood in his exemplar with a *wyn*, misread by him as the Latin letter 'p' which it resembles. Cywa would have been the correct 10th-century latinised version of St Kew's name.

[38] *Itinerary*, ed. L. T. Smith, 1907, I, p. 215.

Two little historical problems are implicit in the very existence of this manuscript at its date. One is how the 10th-century charter found its way into a priory founded, according to its own annals, in 1121; the other is why the Austin canons, having got it, kept it so long. The following solutions are conjectural, as all must be, but fit the facts so far as these are known.

Tradition, according to Leland, attributed to 'Saxon Kinges' the foundation of 'a fre chapelle' having prebendaries at Plympton.[38] No doubt such a tradition existed: an odd legal judgement in the 14th century was based upon it, and it receives further confirmation from the known acquisition of a minster at *Plymentun* by King Edward the Elder.[39] There is therefore nothing inherently improbable in the Cornish belief that King Edgar, too, had interested himself in the welfare of Plympton minster. There was certainly a college of secular canons at Plympton in late Saxon times, for they are mentioned in Domesday Book (as they also were, disapprovingly, in the now lost cartulary of Plympton Priory).[40] That college was abolished by Bishop William Warelwest, a reformer of such institutions. As Leland rather unkindly put it: 'One William Warwist, Bisshop of Exester, displeasid with the chanons or prebendaries ... because they wold not leve theyr concubines, found meanes to dissolve their college, wherin was a deane or provost and 4 prebendaries with other ministers ... Then he set up at Plympton a priorie of canons regular ...'[41] If, as the Cornish in effect asserted, King Edgar had given Lanow church and its land to the canons of that Saxon college, then his charter of donation would certainly once have been preserved at Plympton. It is true that the canons had lost this Lanow church glebe before 1066, as Domesday Book shows; but they would not therewith have also lost the contents of their muniment chest at Plympton. As long as hope of restitution remained they would have treasured that charter, perhaps even reconstructing it if harm befell. When the Austin canons took possession of the demesnes and premises vacated by the retreating canons-secular they must surely have inherited the charters relating to their new possessions at Plympton. We may easily believe that this Lanow charter was among the others. But the Austin canons would have had quite a different motive from their predecessors for preserving such a charter as this (in

---

[39] Oliver, *op. cit.*, p. 129 *n.*; Birch, *Cartularium Saxonicum*, II, no. 610.

[40] DB IV, p. 79; Bodleian MS. James 23 (*Summary Catalogue*, no. 3860), p. 165, a note taken from the cartulary in 1627.

[41] Leland, *loc. cit.*

whatever version). For them it was no longer a title-deed—their title to Lanow church was the charter of Bishop William and its confirmation by King Henry II. The Saxon charter, however, would have afforded a valuable warranty of the antiquity and extent of their newly acquired glebe at Lanow, which, rightly or wrongly, every one seems to have identified with the land King Edgar gave. Doubtless it was this evidential value that saved the charter from complete destruction at the canons' hands during the protracted controversy when (if it said what Cornishmen alleged to be the facts) it was becoming an embarrassment, even a danger, to them. All they required of it was the record of the royal gift of land to the church of Lanow and of its extent; from their point of view the less the charter said about any canons of Plympton and conditions of gift the better. Those were the very things from which they were trying desperately to dissociate their tenure of Lanow church. The chief defects of the text seem likely to be due to the suppression of these awkward particulars, no doubt with some rather clumsy connecting up of mutilated passages.

An alternative hypothesis is that King Edgar made his donation not to the clergy of Plympton but (as the charter could imply) to those of Lanow church, who preserved the document there until the Austin canons came and carried it off to Plympton *c.*1123; and that later Cornishmen merely confused the chronology of these events. Admittedly this alternative greatly improves the integrity of the Grant section of the text: it could be presumed to be substantially accurate, save for the suppressed conditions of the donation. But unfortunately this simple account of the charter's history conflicts with what little evidence there is—the positive evidence of the 1302 assize, and the negative evidence of Domesday Book. The control of Lanow church by a 'foreign' Devonshire community is not likely to have been welcomed by the Cornish of the locality, and it is odd that this imposition should have been attributed to the benefactor of Lanow church, King Edgar, if in fact the culprit was really Bishop William Warelwast. Cornishmen at the 1302 assize knew about the bishop's gift of Lanow church to Plympton Priory; they had his charter before them. Yet they insisted that the king, not the bishop, originated the connection between the two places. The second objection to this hypothesis is that if the charter was preserved from 961 to *c.*1123 at an independent, royally chartered, land-owning, collegiate Cornish church, then that establishment ought to be listed in Domesday Book, but is not, though other collegiate Cornish churches of comparable or less endowments are named, such as those of St Achebran, St Probus, St Carentoch, St Pieran, St Constantine, St Berrion, St Niet, and St Michael. The silence of Domesday about Lanow church is a great puzzle: but to assume a major error of omission in the record is a desperate solution. It is more likely that the establishment there was interrupted during the period 1066-86: but if so, what happened to the charter? Lanow church was in the king's hands in 1123, very possibly in consequence of the young count of Mortain's earlier rebellion and forfeiture. This alternative theory may yet be found to be nearer the truth than the one adopted above; but on existing evidence it seems unsafe to prefer it.

The charter, then, on this showing, has been gutted of its main provisions and is a distorted shadow of its real self. That is indeed deplorable; but at least what remains is substantially authentic. Its losses can to some extent be repaired by the aid of Cornish tradition; and it still contains valuable incidental information. Even in its mutilated state the text is a precious addition to the few pre-Conquest Cornish records that have survived in any state at all.

[See now Wendy Davies, 'The Latin charter-tradition in western Britain, Brittany and Ireland in the early medieval period', in *Ireland in Early Medieval Europe. Studies in Memory of Kathleen Hughes*, edited by Dorothy Whitelock and others (Cambridge, 1982), pp. 258-80 (at p. 272); and Lynette Olson, *Early Monasteries in Cornwall* (Woodbridge, 1989), pp. 81-4. The comparative charter material, not available when the above essay was written, makes Olson favour the alternative interpretation outlined in the penultimate paragraph of this essay, whereby the grant was drawn up for the monastery of Sts Docco and Kew in Cornwall, rather than to a forerunner of the later priory at Plympton; furthermore, this would be compatible with the site of the original monastery being at the present churchtown of St Kew, rather than at the farm now called Lanow, as preferred in this essay. Della Hooke, *Pre-Conquest Charter-Bounds of Devon and Cornwall* (Woodbridge, 1994), pp. 33-7, attempts to trace the bounds on the ground. O.J.P.]

2

THE MANOR OF TREMARUUSTEL
AND THE HONOUR OF ST KEUS

Journal of the Royal Institution of Cornwall, n. s., 7 (1973-7), 220-30.

A PERPLEXING SAINT AND CHURCH; a mysterious honour; one of its component manors, named yet still unidentified: here are deplorable gaps in our understanding of the Exeter Domesday Book when it writes of some place in Cornwall, *Tremaruustel … hec mansio e[st] de honore s[ancti] Chei*;[1] that is (allowing for the ordinary transliteration of initial 'K' for 'Ch' in this manuscript, and restoring to its nominative the genitive case-ending of the saint's name), 'Tremaruustel … this manor is [a member] of the honour of St Keus'.

This study is an attempt to answer the questions, Where was this Manor? What was this honour? Who was this saint? It falls into three parts corresponding to manor, honour and saint's name, but the three problems are linked together and overlap. What throws light upon one of them illuminates the others also.

The Manor of Tremaruustel

This appears in the Exeter Domesday Book (Exon.DB) as a small manor of two acres assessment, with another two acres of woodland and pasture. Edmar had held it in 1066: in 1086 the Count of Mortain (lord of Cornwall) owned it and his tenant, Wihomar, was in occupation. The manor's annual value had declined from 10s. in 1066 to 30d. currently. Having thus declared that this manor was in secular ownership and tenancy, Exon.DB added the cryptic postscript quoted above—'This manor is of the honour of St Keus'. Such postscripts usually indicate that a manor was litigious or usurped. If usurped, its name normally reappeared in the list of *terrae occupatae*, 'usurped lands'. But *Tremaruustel* does not: it receives no further mention. Consequently it is not

[1] DB IV, 225.

clear what the author of this postscript intended to convey by it. The Count was a notorious expropriator of clerical lands; some of which, however, retained a more or less tenuous connection with their former landlords. But no 'Honour of St Keus' is named elsewhere in Cornish records.

Tremaruustel has never been identified satisfactorily. The only clue in Exon.DB to its location is that its name occurs in a group of manors situated in the eastern parts of Cornwall. Only one of the attempts to identify it need detain us; and that not on its merits, but because of the publicity it has received through publication in Canon Thomas Taylor's translation of Exon.DB.[2] He there identified *Tremaruustel* with the medieval manor of Trenance Austell (formerly just *Trenant*, the parochial suffix Austell being added to distinguish it from other Cornish manors called Trenant). But Canon Taylor advanced no substantial arguments for this identification, which seems insufficiently supported. Trenance Austell manor was not in eastern Cornwall; *Tremar-* does not much resemble Trenant (a name which the Exon.DB scribes in Cornwall spelt correctly on six occasions[3]); and while the element *-uustel* might afterwards be spelt *gustel, wustel, wo-stel,* or something similar, it should not, according to rule, become *-austel*. There seems to be equally little substance in the resemblance which Canon Taylor thought he detected between the name of the eponym of a parish church near St Austell, St Ewe *(Sancta Euwa* 1292, *Sancta Ewa* 1282[4]), and the name Keus which, however, he cited in its Exon.DB spelling *Chei,* leaving the Latin genitive case-ending there uncorrected.

But Canon Taylor is only one of many students who have vainly searched for *Tremaruustel* in mid-Cornwall. This misdirection has been due to a passage in the record known as the Geld Inquest, a document contemporary, or nearly so, with the Domesday survey, to which it is prefixed in the Exon.DB manuscript. In the section of the Geld Inquest dealing with the hundred of *Tibesten* (the hundred afterwards called Powdershire) the existence is mentioned of a landowning church which the MS. calls *s[an]c[tu]s Che*;[5] but this is the nominative case of the name, as the terminal letter 's' of *sanctus*, and indeed the grammar of the passage, prove. It has too readily been assumed that this

---

[2] T. Taylor, *Victoria County History of Cornwall*, pt. 8, p. 89 and note.
[3] DB IV, 91, 203, 205, 209, 230, 232.
[4] CRO, Edgcumbe MSS, Bodrugan Cartulary; Hingeston-Randolph, *Bronescombe*, 253.
[5] DB IV, 66.

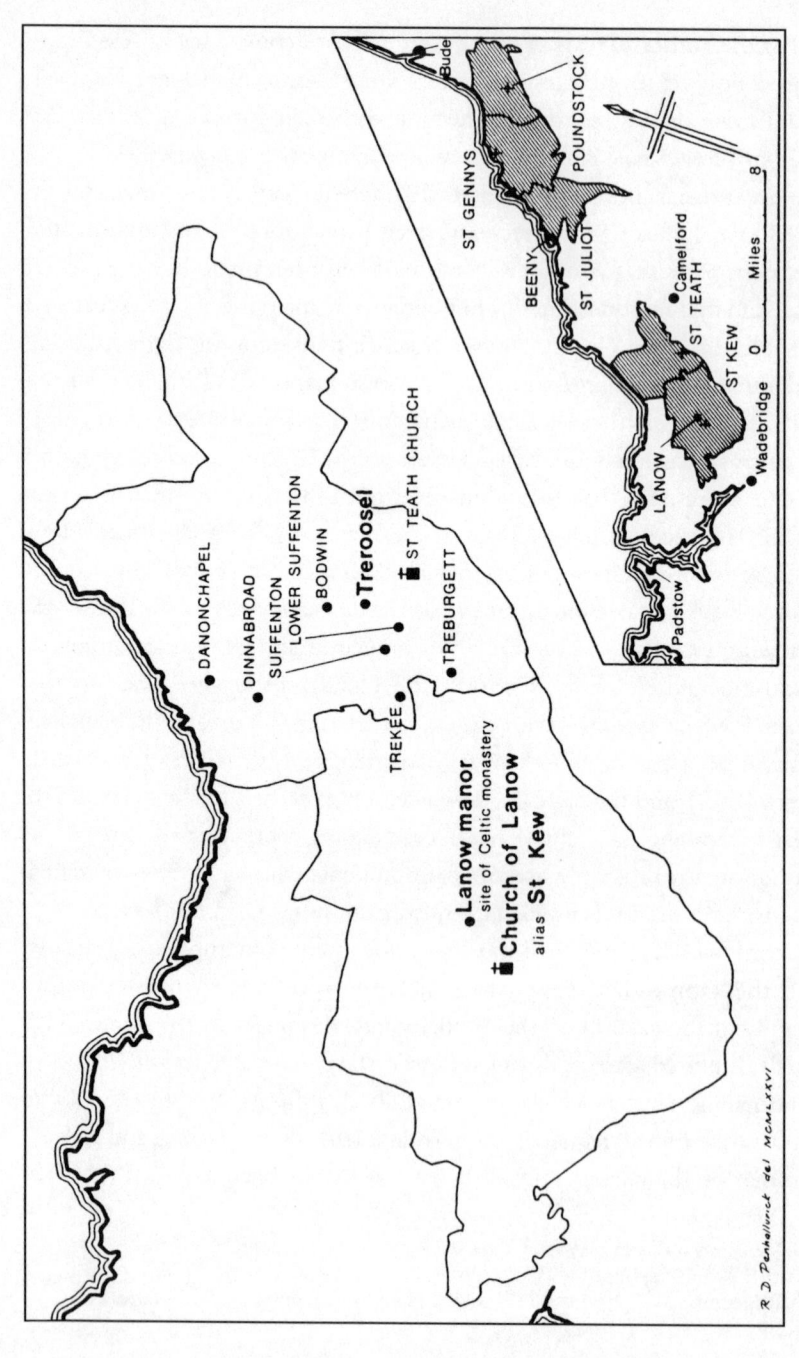

Lanow; Treroosel and area.

St Ke of the Geld Inquest is identical with the St Keus of the Tremaruustel entry in Exon.DB; and this assumption, by misdirecting attention to mid-Cornwall, has like a delusive Will-o'-the-Wisp led students into a morass of unprofitable conjectures. Even Charles Henderson, after demonstrating that St Ke of the Geld Inquest was the eponym of the church of St Kea or Kay near Truro, went on to search for *Tremaruustel* in that vicinity. He could not find it there and had to write 'Tremaruustel does not seem to exist today'.[6] But if this misleading passage in the Geld Inquest is ignored and Exon.DB allowed to speak for itself, investigations at once become productive.

The Exon.DB lists *Tremaruustel* as the penultimate manor in a section of the MS containing names of places in the two hundreds at that time called *Straton* and *Rilleston*. They included, broadly, most of Cornwall to the east of a line from the estuary at Padstow on the north coast to the mouth of the Seaton river on the south coast. Within this area, in what afterwards became the parish of St Teath, is a place now called Treroosel, the early spellings of which name show that it can be the phonological descendant of the Exon.DB Old-Cornish place-name *Tremaruustel*. These earlier spellings of Treroosel are *Trewoosel* 1748,[7] *Trewosall* 1708;[8] *Trewosell* 1546, 1458;[9] *Trerosel* 1316;[10] *Trewosel* 1302, 1284,[11] and *Trewrosel* 1348, 1284.[12] This last is a Middle-Cornish spelling and brings us within sight of the Old-Cornish spelling in Exon.DB. To bridge the gap between these two spellings, *Trewrosel* 1284 and *Tremaruustel* 1086, we must approach them from the Domesday side.

The late Robert Morton Nance suggested to me (letter, 29 December 1955) that *Tremaruustel* belonged to that common class of Cornish place-name, compounded of the word *trev* and a personal name which, in this case, he thought might be *Marchuuist(e)l*, with the 'ch' already silent. *March*, he pointed out, was a common first element of 10th-century Cornish names; while *gustel* and *uuistel* are other spellings of the word *guistel* which is found in the 12th-century Old-Cornish Vocabulary.

[6] CSS, no. 20, p. 32 (*Four Saints of the Fal*, 1929).
[7] Martyn's map.
[8] RIC, PE/16/120.
[9] TM, III, 129; DCRS, *Feet of Fines, Cornwall*, II, no. 1119.
[10] Hingeston-Randolph, *Stapeldon*, 510.
[11] PRO, Just.1/117, *m.* 27; Just.1/111, *m.* 15.
[12] *Anc.D*, IV, A.9234; PRO, Just.1/111, *m.* 15.

It may be so; but I prefer Doble's derivation of *Tremaruustel* from the personal name *Arguistil*, found early in Wales and later at Sant-Allouestre (*Argoestle* 1280) in Brittany.[13] Morton Nance thought it an easy and natural step from the Domesday spelling *Tremaruustel*, through some intermediate form such as Trevrustel, to *Trewrosel* 1284. It is important to notice that the vowel-sound represented in *Tremaruustel* by the letters 'uu' became in *Trewrosel* 1284, and subsequent spellings of this place-name, represented by the Cornish long 'o', as the modern form, Treroosel, clearly indicates.

Phonologically, therefore, Treroosel in St Teath parish can represent the Exon.DB *Tremaruustel*. But are there other Cornish place-names which might do so? There are, in fact, two others which may possibly have a similar origin, namely Trussall in Wendron parish *(Trewrosel* 1327)[14] and Trusell in Tremaine parish *(Trewostel* 1284).[15] Fortunately there are other factors besides etymological ones to aid our judgement. Trussall in Wendron cannot have been the DB manor of *Tremaruustel* because, besides being in the wrong part of Cornwall, it was not of manorial status in 1086 but was then, as it continued to be throughout the Middle Ages, only a tenement within the great manor of *Henliston* (Helston in Kerrier), a royal demesne manor in 1086.[16] Nor is Trusell in Tremaine (though in the right part of Cornwall) eligible, for similar reasons: in 1086 it lay within the royal manor of *Pennehel* (Penheal in Egloskery), of which it was still a tenement held in socage in 1589.[17] Such historical objections do not apply to Treroosel in St Teath, whose medieval history is obscure but which emerges into view in the 16th century as a small manor that had lately belonged to the priory of Launceston,[18] the same kind of status as the DB manor of *Tremaruustel* had. So we may provisionally accept the identification of DB *Tremaruustel* with Treroosel, support for which conclusion will be found in the next section of this study.

---

[13] G. H. Doble, *Saint Dubricius*, 'Welsh Saints' series no. 2 (Guildford, 1943), pp. 17, 18. [Reprinted in G. H. Doble, *Lives of the Welsh Saints*, edited by D. Simon Evans (Cardiff, 1971), pp. 70-1. O.J.P.]

[14] PRO, E.179/87/7, *m*. 3.

[15] PRO, Just.1/ 111, *m*. 37.

[16] DB IV, 92. Cf. manorial surveys in 1337 (PRO, E.120/1, *m*. 16., printed in *The Caption of Seisin of the Duchy of Cornwall*, edited by P. L. Hull, DCRS, n. s. 17 (1971), 88), and *c*.1552 (PRO, E.315/416, p. 26).

[17] DB IV, 94; also survey in 1589 (PRO, SC.11, roll 152).

[18] A. L. Rowse, *Tudor Cornwall* (1941), 218; TM III, 129; PRO, SC.6, Henry VIII, 454. The terrier of the reorganised manor of *Lanovzant* in 1706 is misleading (TM II, 91).

The Honour of St Keus

The search for this honour must now be directed to the district about Treroosel in St Teath. In 1086 and in the following centuries there was, in what became the adjacent parish of St Kew, a large manor taking its name from its capital there at the place now called Lanow.[19] In Exon.DB this manor of *Lannohoo*[20] evidently included most of what became St Kew parish,[21] much of what became St Teath,[22] and a considerable portion of the more distant parish of St Juliot.[23] This great extent explains the assessment of *Lannohoo* in DB at no less than five hides, with woodland one league long by three furlongs wide, one acre of meadow, and 40 acres of pasture.[24] Nor had this been all, for DB tells us that from this manor had already been taken two others, *Podestot* (Poundstock) and *Sainguinas* (St Gennys),[25] which lie, respectively, some 17 and some 14 miles away to the north-east of Lanow. A manor whose ramifications had formerly spread over five later parishes must have been a notable estate in its day. There can be little doubt that in these passages DB is describing parts of the disintegrating territories of the suppressed Celtic monastery of Lanow (originally *Lan-docco*), the earliest Cornish monastery of which we have any documentary record.[26] This once important institution had been suppressed by the Saxons, perhaps by king Edgar who certainly disposed of some of its lands.[27] But the demesnes around the capital at Lanow itself were reserved by subsequent rulers in Cornwall to their own use: both Saxon Harold and Norman William, like their successors, held Lanow manor in demesne.[28] If we are looking for a group of estates which might be thought to constitute an honour, here, centred at Lanow manor, is something very like one, close to Treroosel.

---

[19] This modern spelling is used to avoid confusion, except when italics indicate a quoted version.
[20] DB IV, 92: a mis-spelling of Landohou, originally Lan-docco.
[21] TM, II, 115f.
[22] See Appendix and cf. rental, TM II, 121. St Teath Church was styled *de Lannoumur* ('Great Lanow' manor) in 1302 (PRO, Just. 1/117, m. 60).
[23] Beeney manor was a member of Lanow manor in 1178 (Pipe Roll Soc., vol. 27; 17, 18, printing *Bedem*: in the next two vols., this misreading was corrected to *Bedeni*).
[24] DB IV, 92.
[25] DB IV, 93.
[26] In the earliest *Vita Samsonis*, written perhaps early in the seventh century.
[27] See chapter 1, above.
[28] DB IV, 92 and later records.

Yet there are difficulties in the way of accepting Lanow manor and its affiliated territories as 'the honour of St Keus'. Lanow manor must have been in secular hands for more than a century before 1086, whereas the expression 'the honour of St Keus' had a distinctly ecclesiastical connotation in this Celtic part of England. The Exon.DB uses the term 'honour' of Cornish lands only three times: once of the lands of the canons of St Petroc;[29] once of the lands of the canons of St Piran;[30] and in this instance. Moreover, neither St Keus nor any saint except its founder, St Dawe (*Docco*),[31] is known to have been associated with the Celtic monastery at Lanow[32] or, possibly by tradition, with the supplanting secular manor there.

But if, rejecting Lanow manor and its former dependencies, we have to look again for 'the honour of St Keus', we need not look far. Only half a mile from the site of Lanow manor house, where the ancient monastery had been, a church stood in 1086 beside a Celtic chapel.

In the 10th century this church was a Saxon minster which King Edgar had made collegiate and endowed out of Lanow's ex-monastic lands.[33] This minster, when it had become a Norman parish church, was so environed by the lands of the great manor of Lanow that until the beginning of the 15th century it was usually called the church of *Landoho*, or of *Lanou*, early spellings of Lanow. From the time of the dissolution of the Celtic monastery of Lanow, not later than the middle of the 10th century and perhaps considerably earlier, this Saxon minster must have been the religious centre of the locality. It acquired a collegiate constitution with two residentiary canons; it became endowed with lands by a king; and it possessed the relics of the two most venerated local saints, St Kew and St Dawe (*Docco*), founder of the extinguished Celtic monastery nearby. At first the shrine of St Kew was a chapel in the cemetery of this minster[34] (an interesting circumstance to which I shall return); but by the end of the 14th century this chapel was becoming dilapidated[35] and St Kew's altar was subsequently moved into the adjacent parish church,

---

[29] DB IV, 221, *Lancharet*.
[30] DB IV, 220, *Tregrebri*.
[31] Docco, becoming in Cornwall Dochou, Dohou and finally Dawe.
[32] From Lan-docco, becoming Landochou, Landoho, Landho, Lanou and Lanow.
[33] See note 27.
[34] TM II, 273f.: see also Hingeston-Randolph, *Brantyngham*, 145.
[35] TM, *ibid*.

which thenceforth was called St Kew's Church[36] instead of the church of Lanow (but see below). I have no doubt that the phrase in Exon.DB, 'the honour of St Keus', is nothing but a blunder for 'the honour of St Kew'. In the next section of this study I shall show how easily this blunder could have arisen from the conventional Latinity of 11th-century scribes. Meanwhile we may observe that if the expression 'the honour of St. Keus' in Exon.DB did indeed refer to the former possessions of this collegiate Saxon minster, then the term 'honour' is there employed in exactly the same way as in the other two instances of its use in Cornwall.

But this minster had lost its independent land-owning status, and therefore presumably the collegiate character given to it by King Edgar, before 1086 when it is absent from DB's list of landowning collegiate churches in Cornwall. In all probability it had already been engulfed by Earl Harold's great manor of Lanow before the Norman Conquest. Nevertheless the Normans afterwards made at least partial restitution. At some date, probably after 1123[37] and certainly before King Henry II granted his Confirmation charter to Plympton Priory *c.*1158[38] (in which the Cornish church is stated to be again collegiate), the old constitution bestowed by King Edgar was restored to the church of Lanow. Under King Edgar the maintenance of that college had been entrusted to the Saxon secular canons of Plympton minster: under King Henry I and his reforming bishop of Exeter, William Warelwast, the church of Lanow was given to the Augustinian canons regular of Plympton Priory,[39] who had recently replaced the secular canons.[40] The fate of the territorial endowments of the Saxon collegiate minster of Lanow during the period of its disestablishment is a matter for speculation. If 'the honour of St Keus' refers to those territories, we know what happened to one portion of them, namely *Tremaruustel*. I have already suggested the destiny of the residue, before subinfeudation changed the pattern; and for this opinion I find support in a document whose significance has not, I believe, hitherto been recognised.

---

[36] C. G. Henderson, *Cornish Church Guide* (Truro, 1928), 120.

[37] When Lanow (MS *Tohou* for Dohou) church was given by the king to the bishop and chapter of Exeter cathedral (Mon.Angl., II, 539, Mon.Exon., 134). For discussion of the date of this charter see J. H. Round, *Feudal England* (London, 1895), 482f.

[38] Charter Rolls, 2 Edw. III, *m.* 13; cited in *Mon.Angl.*, VI, 53, and *Mon.Exon.*, 135, num. III.

[39] Hingeston-Randolph, *Bronescombe*, 224.

[40] In 1121; see F. Liebermann, *Ungedruckte anglo-normannische Geschichtsquellen* (Strasburg, 1879), printing *Annales Plymptonienses* (Brit. Mus. MS. 14250).

I give a free translation of it here, where it is relevant; but the Latin text will be found in an appendix to this study.

The document occurs in a manuscript compiled at Plympton Priory, probably in roll format: but its text is known only from a copy of the copy made in the year 1627. Though styled a Register, its contents are not those usual in monastic registers; instead, they consist of excerpts from, or mere references to, title-deeds of properties or privileges of Plympton Priory, together with some declaratory documents like the one we are to consider, forming a collection intended, it is stated, for the use of the priory's procurators when travelling to transact the monks' legal business. The 'register', in fact, is an aide-mémoire for litigation in the priory's interests.

The entry which now concerns us is a statement of a case. From its internal evidence I think it was written during the last quarter of the 12th century, as will be shown in the appendix. The writer, one of the monks of Plympton Priory, declares:

> We are claiming tithes belonging to the church of *Landeho* [Lanow] from seven vills which are in the king's same manor of *Landho* [Lanow], in the vicinity of [saint] Teath's church in Richard Bloiho's fief. Of these [vills] the first is called *Trebridoc* [Treburgett], the second *Trenkioh* [Trekee], the third *Serfonten* [Suffenton], the fourth again *Serfonten* [Lower Suffenton], the fifth *Treursel* [Treroosel], the sixth *Duunaunt* [see note 58], the seventh *Bodwon* [Bodwin]. We have heard from old people that these [tithes] were alienated from *Landeho* [Lanow] church partly because the men of the said vills feared to come to *Landho* church because of blood-feuds arising from a murder, whereas Teath's church was close at hand, but also because the tithes of that period were extremely small and the clergy of *Landho* were powerless [but see note 59] and reluctant to sue for their right. Likewise they neglected to exact from their Franklins the annual Gift and Aid which, it is said, they rightfully were wont to pay. Since then they [the Franklins] pay a small sum, namely one penny from the first acre of a ferlingland, and nowadays nothing more.

What are we to make of the contents of this document? We notice that, though the church of Lanow had been given to Plympton Priory in, or very soon after, 1123, the Austin canons there have to rely in this claim upon hearsay evidence—'We have heard', 'it is said'. Evidently the administrative records of the priory since 1123 contained nothing to support their claim. The document does not say that the Franklins of whom it speaks resided in any of the seven named vills: it is more likely that they were tenants of the glebe of Lanow church—the glebe which the Austin canons of Plympton came to call their manor of Lanow Saint (*Lanou sant*, 'Holy Lanou'), to distinguish it from the secular manor of Lanow, or *Lanoumur* ('Great Lanou'). But this document does bear witness to the existence of a tradition that, at some time long past, Lanow church had suffered loss of tithes from a considerable area within what afterwards became the adjacent parish of St Teath, as well as of other emoluments from its own tenants. That imprecisely remembered event, the cessation of tithes and monetary services formerly rendered by inhabitants of 'the honour of St Kew' to the collegiate minster of Lanow, seems to be the historical heart of this account. That cessation was doubtless caused, not by blood-feuds or negligence, but simply by the transfer of the lands owing those services and tithes from the disendowed minster into the ownership of one or more secular expropriators. It would have been useless for the monks of Plympton to have challenged in the king's courts the acts done by, or with the authority of, his predecessors; hence the story about feuds and negligence, which was feeble but presentable in court. The monks may even have believed it. Some vestiges of those ancient services still survived at the end of the 12th century, it seems: but it is inherently improbable that such a radical transfer of property in that era would ever be completely reversed, even after the re-establishment of the college and despite the complaints of its Augustinian masters. But it can hardly be fortuitous that their traditional legend of an ancient association between Lanow church and Treroosel's neighbourhood accords so remarkably aptly with Domesday Book's linkage of *Tremaruustel* with the 'honour of St Keus', if that honour had indeed belonged to the collegiate Saxon minster of Lanow.

Incidentally it may be observed that, though I have not included the spelling *Treursel* in the 'register' among the examples of early spellings of Treroosel, because this one comes from such a late and inferior source, yet—for what it may be worth—*Treursel*, a late 12th-century spelling if correctly copied, is getting close to that hypothetical spelling Trevrustel (but its letter 'v' would have been *written* 'u', as in *Treursel*) which Morton Nance predicated as an intermediate form between the 1086 Old-Cornish and the 1284 Middle-Cornish versions of this name.

Though all the foregoing considerations justify the hypothesis that there had formerly existed a close (and perhaps vestigially surviving) association between the 11th-century manor of *Tremaruustel* together with an 'honour of St Keus' on the one hand, and the Saxon minster or Norman church of Lanow on the other, its validity must depend upon one essential prerequisite condition; namely, that in late Saxon and early Norman times the cult of St Kew was paramount at Lanow minster. There can be no other reason for an honour belonging to that minster taking St Kew's name. It is the more important to establish the fact of this early paramountcy because the church was not *called* St Kew's church until the 15th century. Previously it had usually been called the church of *Landoho* or *Lanou*, after the secular manor; or sometimes the church of *Lanou saint*, after its own glebe: but in four exceptional instances it had also been called the church of *Tohou*[41] (twice, for *Dohou*), of *sancti Doho*,[42] and, as late as the year 1400, the church of *sancti Doquini*.[43] These are all variants of *Docco,* the original form of St Dawe's name.

We know from King Edgar's charter that St Dawe and St Kew were *both* venerated at this minster in the mid-10th century; but we also know that the former saint's primitive association in this district was with his monastery, on a different site from that of the Saxon minster; while the existence of a shrine of St Kew beside the minster suggests that St Kew's primitive association was with that site. So it is not altogether surprising to discover indications that St Kew's cult was the dominant one at the minster before the 12th century. The bishop and chapter of Exeter Cathedral, who for a short time in 1123 were the owners of Lanow church, were then in process of compiling a martyrology for use in their cathedral. As was the custom, they entered in the martyrology[44] the names of saints connected with places or churches in which they had a special interest. As owners of Lanow church they duly entered St Kew's name on the date of St Kew's feast, 8 February; but they omitted St Dawe's (Docco's or Dohou's) name from his day, 15 February.[45] The implication is that St Kew was then regarded as the principal saint of Lanow

---

[41] In 1123 (see note 37) and 1136 (Hist. MSS. Commission, *Report on MSS in Various Collections,* IV, 43).

[42] [In 1146: D. W. Blake, 'An original bull of Pope Eugenius III, 7th February, 1146', *Devon and Cornwall Notes and Queries,* 34 (1978-81), 307-11; compare *Launceston Cartulary*, edited by Hull, no. 8. O.J.P.]

[43] Hingeston-Randolph, *Stafford*, 271 'Bokelly'.

[44] Exeter Cathedral Chapter MS. 3518.

[45] *Ordinale Exon.*, edited by J. N. Dalton and G. H. Doble, 4 vols., Henry Bradshaw Society, 37-8, 63 and 79 (1909-40), IV, 3-4 and Index of Saints, pp. 44-102; compare p. 41.

church. We find, too, in the 13th and 14th centuries, references to Kew's well in the parish,[46] indicative of a Celtic and possibly enduring cult of the saint; but no well of St Dawe or *Docco* has been recorded. When the Elizabethan hagiographer, Nicholas Roscarrock, a native of that neighbourhood, wrote down his early recollections of the traditions at St Kew's Church, he stated that St Kew was the patron saint of the parish church, while St Dawe was the patron only of a chapel elsewhere in the parish.[47] Indeed, *if* Exon.DB did mean St Kew when it named St Keus, then that is evidence that St Kew's cult at Lanow church was of long-established primacy; for by 1086 the 'honour of St Keus' was in secular hands, its glory already past.

I have mentioned that the shrine of St Kew was a chapel in the cemetery of Lanow church until the early 15th century when St Kew's altar was removed into the enlarged parish church. Such Celtic cemetery chapels were not uncommon. There is an interesting parallel with conditions formerly existing at Wormhout in Flanders.

At Wormhout St Winnoc, a Celt like St Kew, founded a monastery which he named after St Martin. St Winnoc died and was buried at Wormhout, which remained one of the chief centres of his cult throughout the Middle Ages. Until 1736 there stood in the churchyard of St Martin's Church at Wormhout a chapel of St Winnoc.[48] Thus though St Winnoc was the founder of the monastery and church at Wormhout, and was always the chief celebrity there, his actual name was formally attached only to the chapel in the churchyard of his foundation. The analogy with the arrangements at Lanow church is instructive.

The Name Keus

I have still to account for the name *Kew* being miswritten in Exon.DB as Cheus, or rather, in the genitive case of that name, as *Chei*. There is a simple explanation which arises from an orthographic convention adopted by scribes of that period.

The writer with whom this particular mistake originated was presumably the scribe of the Domesday commissioners in the hundred of *Straton*, where

[46] TM II, 139.
[47] Cambridge University Library, Add. MS. 3041, f. 147ᵛ.
[48] CSS, no. 44 (*St Winnoc*) esp. pp. 5, 29 (SC, V, esp. pp. 149-50).

Lanow church was. Now, if the saint of 'the honour of St Keus' was really St Kew, that scribe would have heard the saint's name from the lips of Cornishmen testifying before the commissioners; and the name they uttered would naturally have been no Latinized scribal version of it but the plain vernacular one, which was *Kyw*. *Kyw* or *Cyw* is a Celtic name appearing with a Cornish provenance in two documents, one to be dated *c*.961, the other *c*.1123:[49] it also appears in place-names under Celtic influence outside Cornwall. At this stage let the reader ask himself whether St Kew was a man or a woman. If he is uncertain he should sympathise with the Domesday scribe, who was evidently uncertain too. That scribe was probably a Norman-French speaker, writing in Latin, who was unlikely to have been familiar with the names, still less the genders, of obscure Celtic saints. When he fair-copied his notes for the commissioners he should have Latinized this name as a feminine noun, for St Kew was a woman. He should have tried to represent the name as *Kywa*, or, in the genitive case he needed, as *Kywae* or *Kywe*. Instead he treated the name as a masculine noun whose termination in the nominative case would be 'us', and in the genitive 'i'. But—and this is the crux—instead of writing the name (in his misjudged masculine declension) with its essential letter 'w', or with a conventional 'u' deputising for the 'w', he wrote the utterly misleading spelling *Chei*. The substitution of 'ch' for an initial 'k' is normal practice in Exon.DB; while the change of the 'y' to an 'e' is of no moment: similar substitutions occur in DB spelling of place-names, for example *Cheweshope*, now Cusop in Herefordshire, thought by Professor Ekwall perhaps to contain this same Celtic word *ciu* or *cyw*.[50] But why did our scribe omit the vital equivalent of a letter 'w'? That omission has caused all the confusion, because if a 'w' had been indicated in the name nobody would have overlooked its identification with the name Kew. The reason was in the scribal practice of the period.

When scribes had to add Latin masculine terminations to personal names ending in the letter 'w' they were in a difficulty. There being no letter 'w' in the Latin alphabet they had either to write the 'w' out in full as 'uu', or else, more conveniently, abbreviate it to a single letter 'u'. If they then dutifully added the Latin masculine termination '-us' to such a name the result would

[49] See notes 27 and 45.
[50] DB I, f. 179ᵛ. See also E. Ekwall, *Oxford Dictionary of English Place-Names*, 4th edn. (Oxford, 1960), 137 *Cusop*.

be a word ending either in '-uuus' or '-uus'. Both would be uncouth, and the first one difficult to read in some calligraphies: and that difficulty would be enormously enhanced when an accusative case of the name required the terminations '-uuum' or '-uum'. Very often those repeated minim strokes would make the name unintelligible to the reader. So, when this situation arose, scribes often abated the nuisance by omitting one of the letters 'u'. Celtic names afford many examples of this practice. For instance, the personal name Thethwiw was Latinized as *Thetvius*[51] (instead of Thetviuus); Gwynllyw was Latinised as *Gundleius*[52] (instead of Gundleiuus) and in a later document as *Winleus*[53] (instead of Winleuus); Ubeluiu was written *Ubeluius*[54] (instead of Ubeluiuus); while throughout the *Vita Teliaui* the forms *Telias* and *Teliauus* were used indiscriminately for the nominative case of the name, but the accusative case was always written *Teliaum*[55] (instead of Teliauum).

If our scribe Latinized the name *Kyw* in this way he would have noted down the nominative of the name as *Cheus* (instead of *Cheuus*). But it is obvious that this contracted spelling, *Cheus*, though in accordance with customary practice, is ambiguous: it can represent either of two different Celtic names. As an abbreviation of Keu-us it represents the name *Kyw* (allowing for the mistaken gender); but as an unabbreviated spelling of Ke-us it represents a name like *Ke*. At some very early stage in the compilation of Exon.DB the former intention has been mistaken to be the latter one. As already said, the most likely person to be guilty of this blunder must surely have been the original scribe in *Straton* hundred, who on hearing the feminine name Kyw first of all Latinized it in his notes with that conventionally abbreviated masculine spelling, but who then forgot to remind himself, or perhaps to warn a copyist, that it *was* an abbreviation not to be taken at its face value. From taking it so, by misapprehension, the misleading genitive form of the name, *Chei*, as it stands in Exon.DB, would inevitably be produced.

---

[51] J. Loth, *Les Noms des Saints Bretons* (Paris, 1910), 119.
[52] CSS no. 40 (*St Cadoc*), p. 8; SC, IV, 58. Cf. J. Loth, *Les Mabinogion*, II (Paris, 1913), 290, n. 1.
[53] CSS, no. 11 (*St Petrock*) (3rd edn.) 10, note; SC, IV, 137.
[54] LL, 80.
[55] LL, 97f.

Summary

It appears that there are phonological, topographical and historical justifications for identifying *Tremaruustel* with Treroosel in St Teath parish, and the 'honour of St Keus' with an honour of St Kew belonging to the Saxon minster of Lanow, next St Kew's shrine. There is no difficulty in understanding how St Kew's name came to be misspelt in DB.

The strength of the arguments here advanced lies in the way their several strands are twisted together by DB's single statement about *Tremaruustel* and the 'honour of St Keus'. Manor, honour and saint's name must consequently all be explicable within a single historical context. The identifications and explanations offered in this study will, I believe, be found to satisfy this stringent condition.

I gratefully acknowledge my obligation to Mr. R. D. Penhallurick for the most helpful map.

Appendix

Bodley MS. James 23 (*Summary Catalogue*, no. 3860) is one of a series of notebooks, all extracts in the hand of Richard James from documents and manuscripts. This volume was compiled between 1627 and 1638. It includes on pages 151 to 170 the text of what it calls a 'Register of Plympton' [priory] (*Registrum de Plimtoñ*) taken from a copy supplied in 1627 by the famous Sir John Eliot, M.P. for Cornwall. As it stands in James 23 this text is therefore at least two removes from the original manuscript, even if that was Sir John's exemplar.

A post-medieval copyist, very likely James himself, has slightly altered the spelling that must have characterised the original manuscript, bringing it into conformity with 17th-century scholarship: but this has only involved replacing the medieval feminine termination 'e' by its classical prototype '-ae'; and also substituting the letters 'j' and 'v' for their medieval equivalents 'i' and 'u' whenever it was appropriate to do so. On the other hand, words which were abbreviated in the medieval manner do not appear to have been extended in James 23; though I have done so here for the convenience of readers. One Latin word in the text is obviously misspelt; but it cannot now be known at what stage in this recension of the text that error appeared.

The date of this entry in the 'register' is roughly indicated by its mention of Richard *Bloiho* as lord of the fief which then included St Teath's church.

This Richard, a cadet of the senior line of the great Bloyow family of Cornwall, appears to have flourished during the period *c*.1180-1206. Like his kinsmen, though through a different inheritance, he was a landowner in the parishes of St Endellion and St Teath. But the text printed below was probably penned not later than 1195, for in that year King Richard gave the royal (and erstwhile comital) manor of Lanow to Simon his butler (*pincerna regis*); after which it remained subinfeudated and is not likely to have been described as 'the king's manor' as it is in this text.

A translation will be found on page 20.

Nos vendicamus vij. villarum decimas quarum corpora[56] habemus ad ecclesiam de Landeho. quae sunt in eodem manerio Regis de Landho. adversus Egglostetha,[57] quae est in feodo Ric[ardi] Bloiho. harum prima dicitur Trebridoc . secunda Trenkioh tertia Serfonten . quarta similiter Serfonten . quinta Treursel . sexta Duunaunt . septima Bodwon.[58] Illas ab antiquis audivimus ideo esse alienatas ab ecclesia de Landeho . tantum quia homines dictarum villarum timuerunt venire ad ecclesiam de Landho propter inimicitias homicidii cujusdam . et ecclesia sanctae Tetha [*sic*] prope erat tantum quia decimas illius temporis parvulae erant, et clerici de Landho impoles[59] [*sic*] et pigri jus suum prosequi . Ideo etiam omittebant de Francoleinis suis annuatim donum et auxilium exigere quod ut dicitur illi de jure debebant pendere. Quoniam parvulum censum solvunt scilicet de acra . I°. de ferlingo terrae, unum denarium et modo nil amplius.

---

[56] *Corpus* has many medieval senses; here its plural clearly indicates corporate possessory rights of some kind.

[57] *Egglostetha*, i.e. *eglos Tetha*, 'Teath's Church'.

[58] These seven places were all in St Teath parish. Their modern names are given in the translation above, except that of *Duunaunt* which perhaps represents *deu-nant*. It was spelt *Deunant* in 1262, *Dounant* in 1297 and 1409, and *Daunand* in 1422. This word appears to survive today only as a corrupted prefix to place-names near the valleys, such as Dannonchapel, Dinnabroad, etc. Bodwin, surprisingly, was spelt *Bossewoen* on at least one occasion in 1302, so the termination '-won' in this text may be accurate. It would be wrong to translate *vill* in a 12th-century Cornish context as 'village'; the word, borrowed from English administrative usage, must be given the sense of an undefined but small district.

[59] *Impoles*, a meaningless word, is perhaps a copyist's error for *impotes*, 'powerless'; but there may have been confusion with an abbreviated spelling of *impolitia*, 'negligence', which would be apt.

3
BISHOP WULFSIGE COMOERE:
AN UNRECOGNISED 10TH-CENTURY GLOSS IN THE BODMIN GOSPELS

Cornish Studies, 14 (1986), 34-8

ONE OF THE DIFFICULTIES in establishing the sequence of the 10th-century Cornish bishops has been an apparent conflict of evidence involving a certain Bishop Comoere, or Cemoyre: it is necessary to fit him into the succession at a period when, according to one account, there appears to have been no vacancy for him.

After the death (between A.D. 981 and 988-90) of Bishop Wulfsige of Cornwall, Archbishop Dunstan compiled for King Æthelred II an account of the tenure by successive bishops of some Cornish estates. Dunstan brings his narrative up to date by saying '... King Eadred commanded Daniel to be consecrated, and gave the estates, as the witan advised him, to the bishop-stool at St Germans. Afterwards, when King Edgar bade me consecrate Wulfsige, he and all our bishops said that they did not know who could possess the estates with greater right than the bishop of the diocese ...'.[1] The most natural meaning of this passage, and the one most apt to Dunstan's argument, is that Wulfsige was Daniel's *next* successor in the Cornish episcopate: from which it would follow that Daniel and Wulfsige (who was signing as late as 980-1)[2] between them covered the whole period of King Edgar's reign (959-75). But against this must be set the evidence of various manumission entries in the 10th-century manuscript generally known as the Bodmin Gospels,[3] which show

---

[1] A. S. Napier and W. H. Stevenson, *The Crawford ... Charters*, no. VII. See edition, translation and discussion by Dorothy Whitelock, in *Councils and Synods with other Documents Relating to the English Church*, edited by Dorothy Whitelock and others (Oxford, 1981), pp.165-73.

[2] J. M. Kemble, *Codex Diplomaticus*, nos. DCXXIV and DCXXIX; P. H. Sawyer, *Anglo-Saxon Charters: An Annotated List and Bibliography* (London, 1968), nos. 837 and 838.

[3] British Library, Additional MS. 9381. The most recent edition is by Max Förster, 'Die Freilassungsurkunden des Bodmin-Evangeliars', in *A Grammatical Miscellany Offered to Otto Jespersen*, edited by N. Bøgholm and others (London and Copenhagen, 1930), pp. 77-99.

a certain Bishop Comoere acting in Cornwall in the latter part of that reign.[4] These entries led Stubbs to classify Comoere as a Cornish bishop *tempore regis Eadgari*.[5]

An additional doubt about the meaning of Dunstan's narrative is imported by William of Malmesbury's statement that Bishop Daniel of Cornwall died in the year 956 (some seven years before the first known signature of Bishop Wulfsige).[6] William's evidence, though late, must be received with respect; nevertheless in this instance his date is clearly erroneous, because Daniel was certainly alive and signing as late as 959.[7] Moreover a charter has recently come to light in which Daniel and Oswald appear together among the attesting bishops.[8] This, supposing this witness-list to be authentic, could not have happened before 961, when Oswald was consecrated Bishop of Worcester.[9] I suggest that the real date of Daniel's death was 961 (his obit was said to have been observed on 8 October),[10] and that William of Malmesbury's impossible date, 956, is due to someone misreading DCCCLXI as DCCCLVI. With Daniel's death in 961 the first known signature of Wulfsige in 963 would agree satisfactorily.[11] But, whether or not this is the explanation of the incorrect date in William of Malmesbury's text, it is evident that the only substantial objection to the acceptance of Wulfsige as Daniel's immediate successor is the intrusive presence of Bishop Comoere in the Bodmin Manumissions.

A solution of the difficulty was first suggested, I believe, by Henry Jenner in 1923,[12] and was afterwards accepted by C.G. Henderson.[13] Jenner thought

[4] *Loc. cit.*, ff. 141a *bis*, 141b.

[5] W. Stubbs, *Registrum Sacrum Anglicanum* (1897), p. 28. He misled the compilers of the *Handbook of British Chronology*, 1st and 2nd editions, edited by F. M. Powicke and E. B. Fryde (London, 1941 and 1961), who listed Wulfsige and Comoere as separate bishops; but Dr. Simon Keynes, in the third edition (edited by E. B. Fryde and others, London, 1986), now has Bishop Wulfsige Comoere correctly listed.

[6] John Scott, *The Early History of Glastonbury: An Edition, Translation and Study of William of Malmesbury's 'De Antiquitate Glastoniensis Ecclesie'* (Woodbridge, 1981), p. 138.

[7] W. de G. Birch, *Cartularium Saxonicum*, III, no. 1045 (Sawyer, no. 660); and H. P. R. Finberg, *The Early Charters of Wessex* (Leicester, 1964), no. 483 (Sawyer, no. 652).

[8] See chapter 1, above; Sawyer, no. 810.

[9] The witness-list, including Bishop Daniel, must therefore date from either 961 or 962 (when one of the witnesses, Ealdorman Æthelwold, died).

[10] William of Malmesbury, *loc. cit.*

[11] Birch, *op. cit.*, III, no. 1118 (Sawyer, no. 715).

[12] Henry Jenner, 'The Manumissions in the Bodmin Gospels', *Journal of the Royal Institution of Cornwall*, 21 (1922-5), 235-60, at pp. 252-3.

[13] C. G. Henderson, *The Cornish Church Guide* (Truro, 1925), p. 26.

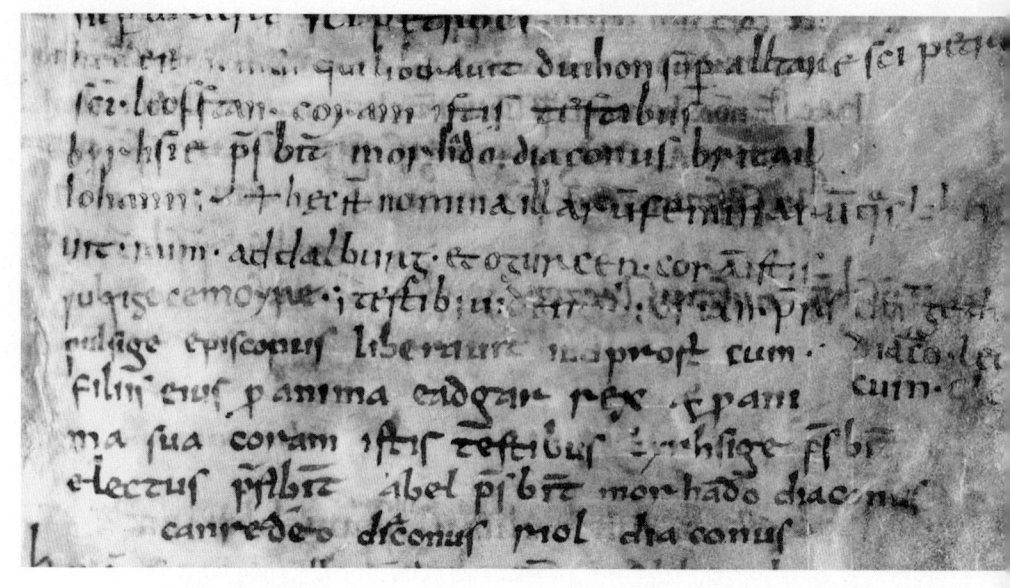

British Library, Additional MS. 9381, the Bodmin Gospels, fol. 1ʳ (detail), reproduced by kind permission of the British Library Board.

that Wulfsige and Comoere were not two bishops but one; and that Wulfsige bore both a Saxon and a Celtic name, *Wulfsige Comoere*, as did *Wulfnoð Rumuncant*,[14] *Ælfeah Gerent*,[15] *Æpælwine Muf*[16] and also (if this is the right reading) *Wunsie Cenmonoc*,[17] Cornishmen who all lived in King Edgar's reign.

It now appears that Jenner was right: the proof of his hypothesis has existed all the time in one of the manumission memoranda in the Bodmin Gospels, but in a passage so generally misread and misprinted that no-one has recognised its significance.

This double name, *Wulsige Cemoyre*, actually occurs in one place among those memoranda,[18] where it has duly been noted by Jenner and others: but

---

[14] Birch, *op. cit.*, III, no. 1197 (Sawyer, no. 755). The lands of this charter, however, were not in Devon (as Birch believed), but in the present parish of St Keverne in Cornwall (so Sawyer, following Henderson and Finberg).

[15] Birch, *op. cit.*, III, no. 1231 (Sawyer, no. 770).

[16] Förster, 'Freilassungsurkunden', no. 22.

[17] G. Oliver, *Monasticon Dioecesis Exoniensis*, p. 433, no. 44. However, Thorpe and others read *Cenmenoc* only (B. Thorpe, *Diplomatarium Anglicum*, p. 626; Förster, 'Freilassungsurkunden', no. 24).

[18] British Library, *loc. cit.*, f. 1a.

Jenner, like almost everyone else, read it as part of the wrong entry—as part, that is, of the memorandum which both precedes and overlaps the one to which the name properly belongs. This misreading can only be made at the cost of making nonsense of the syntax and meaning of the first entry. So unintelligible does the first entry then become, if the name is read with it, that Kemble took upon himself to alter the text, printing it with this name falsely and without warning transposed into the middle of a sentence which, in the manuscript, stands on the line above, not with, the name.[19] Thorpe followed him in printing this false text.[20] Haddan and Stubbs scrupulously printed the sequence of the words as they stand in the manuscript, non-sense notwithstanding;[21] but since by so doing they represented the name to be part of the wrong memorandum, their text is as confusing as the others. Only Dr. George Oliver seems to have recognised that this name ought to be read, not with the preceding and overlapping lines of the entry before it, but with the lines of writing containing the next entry following it (though I cannot agree with him that the handwriting of the name is that of the latter entry);[22] even so, he missed its significance.[23] Stokes similarly inserted the names into the middle of the preceding entry;[24] Förster elevated the two names to an entry in their own right (his no. 6), but wrongly inserted a punctuation mark between them, and claimed that the names represented manumittor and manumitted, thus again missing the true significance of the entry.[25] (He did, however, correctly point out that the hand was distinct from those of the entries preceding and following it.) In fact the calligraphy of the name *Wulsige Cemoyre* is distinctly different from that of either the preceding or the succeeding entry: it is an addition to one or the other of them, and its position makes it quite clear that it is a gloss written over the words *Wulsige episcopus* with which the succeeding entry commences.[26]

[19] Kemble, *op. cit.*, IV, p. 309.
[20] B. Thorpe, *Diplomatarium Anglicum*, p. 623.
[21] A. W. Haddan and W. Stubbs, *Councils and Ecclesiastical Documents*, I, p. 677.
[22] Oliver, *op. cit.*, p. 431 and note.
[23] He lists Wulfsige and Comoere as two bishops on p. 435.
[24] W. Stokes, 'The Manumissions in the Bodmin Gospels', *Revue celtique*, 1 (1870-2), 332-45, at p. 33.
[25] Förster, 'Freilassungsurkunden', no. 6 (p. 84 and note).
[26] Contrast, for example, the *s*, *g* and *m* of the gloss with the *s* of *testib;*, the *g* of *Ogurcen*, and the *m* of *nomina* in the preceding entry; also the word *Wulsige* in the gloss with the same word underneath it in the succeeding entry. The differences of the handwritings are very noticeable.

The calligraphic evidence here is amply confirmed by the manner in which the manumission entries on this part of the page are set out. The three relevant entries are the fourth, fifth and sixth on folio 1a.[27] It is not difficult to see that, of them, the fourth entry was written first, followed, a little way down the page, by the sixth. Subsequently, but not very long afterwards, the gloss *Wulsige Cemoyre* was added over the sixth entry's opening words. The date of the gloss is important, but it can be discussed better after the extract printed below has been read. Last of all the fifth entry was inserted in the space between the other two. Its scribe found himself in trouble, for he had not room enough: the expedients to which he was put in order to cram his entry in have been the cause of all the confusion. What happened can best be shown by setting out the three entries. Although in the manuscript each of these three entries, and also the gloss, is in a different handwriting, it is only necessary for our purpose to distinguish that of the gloss and that of the fifth entry. The gloss is here put arbitrarily in capitals in heavier type, and the fifth entry in italic type. Capital letters have been supplied, but the punctuation is unchanged.

[4th] Hoc est nomen qui liberauit Duihon sup altare sc̃i Petroci sc̃i.[28] Leofstan . coram istis testibus Byrhsie p̃sbīt Morh^aðo diaconus Britail

[5th] Iohann:~ ✝ *Hec s̃t nomina illarũ feminarũ q^as libera uit . Rum . Addalburg . et Ogurcen . corā istis* WULSIGE CEMOYRE *:, testib; uidentib; Osian p̃res̃ Can^tgethen*

[6th] Wulsige episcopus liberauit Iudprost cum   diac̃o . Leu filiis eius p anima Eadgar rex [*sic*] & p ani   cum . cleric̃ ma sua coram istis testibus Byrhsige p̃sbīt Electus p̃sibīt Abel p̃sbīt Morhaðo diaconus Canreðeo di^aconus Riol diaconus

It will be seen that the scribe of the compressed fifth entry endeavoured to keep his handiwork distinct from the other entries by prefacing it with a cross[29] and by separating his third line from the gloss by a bold punctuation sign (of vital significance, but wholly ignored by the editors, who do not print

---

[27] British Library, *loc. cit.*

[28] i.e. *scilicet*.

[29] In these manumissions the infrequent crosses do not necessarily indicate the presence of a bishop.

it). His final words had to be relegated to the margin alongside the following, but earlier written, entry.

The gloss can be dated within a generation. It was written after the sixth entry which it glosses and to which Bishop Wulfsige was a party, and before the fifth entry which it cramps. The fifth entry itself was written in the lifetime of Osian the priest and of Leucum the clerk, two of its witnesses. These men witnessed together other manumissions entered in this book, in particular two: one in the reign of King Eadred (that is, not later than 955) to which *Comuyre* himself, as a priest, was also a witness;[30] the other when *Comoere* was a bishop.[31] They were therefore contemporaries of Comoere both before and after his consecration, and this gloss upon Bishop Wulfsige's name, showing that he was also known as *Wulsige Cemoyre,* was written in their lifetime. Possibly Comoere, who, from his name, must have been a Cornishman, was best known at St Petroc's Cornish monastery by his Celtic name:[32] but after his consecration by command of a Saxon king he may diplomatically have used his Saxon name, Wulfsige.

There remains, then, no reason to doubt that Dunstan, writing to King Æthelred, meant to convey that Bishop Daniel of Cornwall was succeeded by Bishop Wulfsige with no other bishop intervening.[33]

Acknowledgment

The usefulness of this article has been greatly enhanced by additional references supplied by Dr. S. D. Keynes and Mr. O. J. Padel, whose assistance the author gratefully acknowledges.

---

[30] British Library, *loc. cit.*, f. 13a. Förster, 'Freilassungsurkunden', no. 36.
[31] *Loc. cit.*, f. 141a. Förster, 'Freilassungsurkunden', no. 44.
[32] The Old Welsh personal name *Cimuireg* (the *g* silent) is exactly equivalent to *Comoere*: J. Gwenogvryn Evans and John Rhys, *The Text of the Book of Llan Dâv* (Oxford, 1893), pp. 75 and 172; compare also perhaps Old Breton names in *Com-* and *-uuere*: J. Loth, *Chrestomathie bretonne* (Paris, 1890), pp. 119 and 173.
[33] His first known signature as Wulfsige was in 963 (see note 9): it is uncertain if any of his appearances in the Bodmin Manumissions as Bishop Comoere was earlier than this.

4
TREMAIL AND TURGOIL IN DOMESDAY BOOK

Devon and Cornwall Notes and Queries, 36 (1987-91), 269-73

DOMESDAY BOOK (DB) manorial identifications, when supported by subsequent records, may be secure; but those depending upon mere resemblances between DB and later spellings may be open to revision, and of such are the DB manors of *Tremail* and *Turgoil* in Cornwall. They occur in both the Exchequer Domesday Book[1] and the Exeter Domesday Book (Exon.DB)[2] among the list of manors belonging to the canons of St Petroc of Bodmin (St Petroc, for short).

Canon Thomas Taylor, in his translation of the Cornwall part of Exon.DB, makes the cautious suggestions, with question marks, that *Tremail* might be Tremeal (but now usually written Tremail) in the parish of Davidstow, and *Turgoil* might be Tregolds in that of St Merryn.[3] The editors of the Phillimore edition of Domesday Book, in the Cornwall volume, adhere to this identification of DB *Tremail*,[4] but prefer to identify DB *Turgoil* with Tregole in Poundstock parish.[5] Unlike Taylor, they express no doubts. None of these attributions is supported by other records, so we are entitled to review their merits.

TREMAIL IN DAVIDSTOW appears in 18th-century rentals of the manor of Treglasta (DB *Treglastan*) as a free tenement of the manor. The name was usually *Tremeal*—Taylor's spelling of the modern name. In the year 1712 this tenement owed to the lord of Treglasta manor a high rent of one shilling and three pence yearly.[6] In DB the manor was in secular ownership and it remained so thereafter, except for a portion which was given to the Somerset abbey of

---

[1] *Domesday Book seu Liber Censualis*, vol. I (Record Comm. 1783), fol. 120v-121r.
[2] DB, IV, 185 (*Tremail*) and 186 (*Turgoil*).
[3] *Victoria County History: Cornwall*, part 8 (London, 1924), p. 71.
[4] *Domesday Book: Cornwall* (Phillimore), 4, 14.
[5] *Ibid.*, 4, 16.
[6] MS. in the author's possession [now in the RIC, Truro. O.J.P.].

Cleeve in the 13th century. There seems to be nothing in other records to indicate that St Petroc ever had or claimed land in Davidstow parish.

TREGOLE IN POUNDSTOCK parish, near the boundary with Lesnewth parish, was a tenement of Lesnewth manor as late as 1823,[7] by which time ancient manors had commonly lost many of their free tenements. Evidently Tregole was an important part of Lesnewth manor, for at that date it comprised eight free tenements.

Lesnewth manor was relatively small, but it was ancient and important. It was the chief manor in the hundred of Lesnewth when that was carved out of the DB hundred of *Straton*, and to it was annexed the bailiwick of the hundred court. It is likely that Tregole belonged for many centuries to Lesnewth manor, whose medieval owners lived in Devon[8] and showed little activity in their Cornish estate. Neither in Poundstock nor in Lesnewth parish did St Petroc claim lands. So much for the lack of supporting *prima facie* evidence why either Tremail in Davidstow or Tregole in Poundstock should be identified with one or other of DB *Tremail* and DB *Turgoil*. It is, of course, negative evidence, not to be stressed: but it exists.

TREGOLDS IN ST MERRYN is a different matter. Here there are positive reasons for rejecting an identification with St Petroc's manor of Turgoil. Tregolds (formerly Tregoll and Tregollas), with the whole parish of St Merryn and several others, lay within the huge episcopal manor of Pawton (DB *Pauton*). It is recorded that *Polltun*, or Pawton manor, was one of the Cornish estates which King Egbert gave to the bishop of Sherborne in the ninth century.[9] Thereafter the manor descended to successive bishops who were responsible for Cornwall. At the date of the Domesday Book survey Pawton manor belonged to the Bishop of Exeter,[10] whose successors retained it until the 16th century. The peculiarity of that episcopal tenure was this, that there is every reason to think the whole of this great manor had originally been ravished by King Egbert from the Celtic monks of St Petroc. So that, in respect of this manor with its tenement of Tregolds, the bishop and St Petroc were, historically, rivals.

---

[7] TM, II, 403.
[8] Dennys of Orleigh, co. Devon: see TM, II, 402.
[9] *The Crawford Charters*, ed. Napier and Stevenson, no. 7.
[10] DB, IV, 181.

A less probable identification than that of St Petroc's manor of Turgoil with the bishop's tenement of Tregolds in Pawton manor can hardly be suggested.

It is, however, possible to proffer probable identifications of DB *Tremail* and DB *Turgoil*. In the Exon.DB list of St Petroc's manors in Cornwall the two named *Tretdeno* and *Botcinnu* are placed next to one another.[11] They are respectively Treknow and Bossiney, both in the parish of Tintagel. In 1337[12] and 1650[13] both were tenements of the manor of Tintagel (which was, indeed, at first called the manor of Bossiney). The conflation of these two DB manors suggested to the present writer that perhaps other DB manors of St Petroc might have done the same: the idea was worth testing. Rather to the writer's surprise the tests showed that the sequences in which St Petroc's manors were listed in Exon. DB were highly suggestive of this process. They were entered (as it proved) in sequences derived from the hundreds of Cornwall, with the addition of a composite list made for another purpose. The sequences were as follows. First, by right of its capital status as the site of St Petroc's collegiate church (though it breaches the hundred sequence which is implicit in this list), is the manor of *Bodmine*.[14] Then follow the names of 11 manors, all identifiable, in the DB hundred of *Pauton*, later called Pydarshire, where the bulk of St Petroc's estates were situated.[15] Next come four manors of which the first two, DB *Tretdeno* and DB *Botcinnu*, are known to have been in the DB hundred of *Straton*, and so was the fourth manor, DB *Polroda* (Polrode in St Tudy parish).[16] It is a fair inference that the intermediate third manor, our DB *Tremail*,[17] was in the same DB hundred. These four are followed by two more manors of which the second one, DB *Fosnewit*,[18] has been safely identified with Bodmin priory's manor of Fursnewth in the parish of St Cleer. It was in the DB hundred of *Fauuiton* or Fawiton, later called West Wivelshire. But

---

[11] DB, IV, 185.

[12] *Caption of Seisin of the Duchy of Cornwall*, ed. P. L. Hull, DCRS, n. s., vol. 17, p. 30 (*Trenou*) and p. 32 (*Boscini*).

[13] *Parliamentary Survey of the Duchy of Cornwall*, part 2, ed. Norman J. G. Pounds, DCRS, n.s., vol. 27, p. 180 (*Bosiney*) and p. 182 (*Trenow*).

[14] DB, IV, 183.

[15] DB, IV, 183-5.

[16] DB, IV, 186.

[17] DB, IV, 185.

[18] DB, IV, 186.

whether or not the preceding manor, our DB *Turgoil*,[19] ought to be reckoned with DB *Fosnewit* in that hundred or with DB *Polroda* and its fellows in their hundred remains uncertain until later records about Fursnewth settle the matter, as will be shown. Last in the sequence of St Petroc's manors comes a composite list of 10 estates,[20] all of them reappearing later in the Exon.DB under the heading *Terrae Occupatae*, 'Usurped Lands'.[21]

The clue given by the amalgamation of DB *Tretdeno* and DB *Botcinnu* can now be followed. If these two adjacently named manors could unite, why not others too? What about the unknown DB *Tremail* and DB *Polroda*, for instance?

TREVILLEY IN ST TEATH. The difference between the DB name *Tremail* and the name of Trevilley, a tenement of the manor of Polrode from at least the 14th century, is more apparent than real. The earlier form of the name Trevilley was *Trevely*; but mutation, as here, may change the letter 'm' in Cornish place-names to the letter 'v' in certain circumstances. *Trevely* is named as a tenement of Polrode manor in a rental of 1598;[22] and a comparison of that rental with one of 1385 shows that the damaged tenement-name *Treu*... in the latter must have represented *Trevely*.[23] Polrode manor itself seems to have lost its DB link with St Petroc in subsequent centuries—in 1301 it was being held of the earl of Cornwall's honour of Launceston castle by the service of six knights' fees;[24] yet the lord of Polrode owed a high rent of 14 pence yearly in 1545 for *Trevely* to the manor of Pendavey.[25] Until Bodmin priory was dissolved, its manor of Pendavey had been a collecting point for scattered rents in north Cornwall.

Nor was Trevilley the only tenement of Polrode manor to have been associated with St Petroc. The inquisition taken in 1305 after the death of Alan Bloyou, lord of *Polroda* manor, records that he held *Tregonwithen* of the prior of Bodmin.[26] This name, *Tregonwithen*, has become Tregwethen, a steading in the parish of St Teath adjoining its churchtown and possibly of older origin

---

[19] DB, IV, 186.
[20] DB, IV, 186-7.
[21] DB, IV, 470-1.
[22] Trelawny Register 'Polrode manor'.
[23] Extent of *Polroda*, Brit. Lib., Add. Charter 64509.
[24] *Cal. of Inquisitions post mortem*, IV, no. 604 (Inq. p. m. of Edmund, Earl of Cornwall).
[25] PRO, C142/70/5 (Inq. p. m. of John Skewys).
[26] *Cal. of Inq. p. m.*, vol. IV, no. 379.

than the latter (though not than its church of which the prior of Bodmin was the patron in the year 1258[27]). In rentals of Polrode manor, especially in the fine series extending over the 18th century,[28] several tenements bear the names *Tregwethen* and *Trewethen* (with *Tregwethen* predominating). Although both of these spellings occasionally occur as names of different tenements in a rental, as if they were different place-names, the Tithe map and Apportionment of St Teath show that in 1840 all such tenements formed a group of fields at Tregwethen, next the churchtown.[29] It is possible that the variant spelling *Trewethen* in these records was due to the influence of the place named Trewethen which was only a mile distant from Tregwethen in St Teath, but was in the parish of St Kew and its manor of Lanowmur.

The 14th-century manor of *Polroda* had become far larger than the DB manor of that name through the incorporation into it of a number of local manors belonging to the Bloyow family (hence the service of six knights' fees in 1301). In consequence the tenements of this manor, feudally considered, were something of a rag-bag, owing services to a variety of other landlords. Trevilley and Tregwethen were examples of this.

TRENGALE IN ST CLEER PARISH appears as *Trengala* among the tenements of Fursnewth manor (DB *Fosnewit*) in a list made in 1485 when that manor still belonged to Bodmin priory.[30] Evidently Trengale represents DB *Turgoil*, which had become amalgamated with the adjacently written DB *Fosnewit* manor, just as the next preceding pair in the Exon.DB list, DB *Tremail* and DB *Polroda*, had amalgamated, and the pair listed next before again, DB *Tretdeno* and DB *Botcinnu*, had done the same.

These sequences of St Petroc's DB manors, *Tretdeno, Botcinnu, Tremail*, and *Polroda*, all in the DB hundred of *Straton*, and of the DB manors of *Turgoil* and *Fosnewit*, both in the hundred of *Fawiton*, coupled with the sequence of the saint's manors in the DB hundred of *Pauton* (as described above), illustrate the use made of the returns from the hundreds of Cornwall by the compilers of the Exeter Domesday Book.

[27] *Register of Bishop Bronescombe*, ed. F. C. Hingeston-Randolph (London, 1889), p. 178.
[28] Cornwall Record Office, Boconnoc Estate MSS.
[29] Cornwall Record Office.
[30] Devon Record Office, Exeter, CR 655. The damaged regnal year can be ascertained from internal evidence.

5
CORNISH PLACE-NAMES AND FIEFS IN A 12TH-CENTURY CHARTER

Cornish Studies, 13 (1986), 55-61

IN 1899 J. H. ROUND printed a series of charters and abstracts of charters relating to the properties belonging to Bernard, a scribe of King Henry I.[1] The first charter so printed was dated by Round as 'previous to 1123'.[2] It contains a list of Bernard's Cornish lands and benefices with the names of their several feudal overlords. These feudal particulars give the document its peculiar historical importance and it is with them alone that this article is concerned.

During the century following the Domesday Book survey in 1086 the feudal organisation of Cornwall underwent radical change. For example, an earldom of Cornwall had come into existence which differed in various respects from the lordship of Cornwall enjoyed by Count Robert of Mortain in 1086, not least because most of the manors which then had been demesne of the Crown had become demesne of the earldom. Moreover manors which Count Robert himself had held in demesne, or which a number of his immediate sub-tenants had held of him, had, as it were, been shuffled and dealt again after the possessions of Count Robert's son and successor, Count William of Mortain, had been forfeited to the king after the count's overt rebellion in 1106.[3] But it is noteworthy that, though so many of the count's Cornish tenants thus lost their estates, his three Cornish barons retained their fiefs almost or wholly unimpaired. They must have avoided implication in their overlord's treason. Indeed in two of those baronies, the ones known to us as the baronies of Trematon and Cardinan, descendants of their Domesday Book tenants continued to rule for two centuries. The third barony, Bodardel, had become

---

[1] J. H. Round, 'Bernard, the king's scribe', *English Historical Review*, 14 (1899), 417-30.
[2] *Ibid.*, p. 420.
[3] His lands had been sequestrated in 1104.

united with that of Cardinan before 1175 when a certain Lady Agnes had carried it in marriage to Robert fitz William, the third Baron of Cardinan. She was probably a descendant of Turstin who had held the manors and fees of the barony of Bodardel in 1086.[4] The civil war of Stephen's reign may have added its quota to the disruption of the existing feudal order in Cornwall, as the chronicler implies,[5] though possibly less permanently than might be supposed, because Count Alan's measures in 1140 were transitory and the harassment of the king's supporters by Earl Reginald and his father-in-law, the Baron of Cardinan, were probably followed by some restitution after the war when the conflicting parties had to live together in peace if not in amity. Moreover Earl Reginald had to win absolution from the excommunication earned by his ravages during the war, though that penalty is more likely to have been incurred by his ecclesiastical than by his secular depredations.[6] He had, for example, demolished the tower of the church of St Stephen by Launceston:[7] his subsequent benefactions of its owners, the Austin Canons of St Stephen, were perhaps part of his atonement. In consequence of these disturbances almost all the lesser than baronial fiefs in Cornwall which are discernible in Domesday Book are later found distributed differently in new fiefs belonging to tenants of whose names the Domesday Book knows nothing.[8] This process reached its culmination during the rule of Earl Reginald, 1140-1175, at whose death the feudal structure of Cornwall had become moulded into the shape which it retained, with little modification, throughout the remainder of the Middle Ages.[9]

This feudal reorganisation of Cornwall during the years between 1086 and 1175 was thus of fundamental importance in the county's territorial and constitutional history: unfortunately it is also very obscure. Between Domesday Book in 1086 and the *Carta* of Earl Reginald in 1166 very few records elucidating that process have survived; and of those few this charter is the

---

[4] Shown by comparison of DB tenures with later known fees of the honours of Cardinan and Bodardel.

[5] *Gesta Stephani*, ed. K. R. Potter (London, 1955), p. 67.

[6] *Ibid.*, p. 68.

[7] *Launceston Cartulary*, no. 13.

[8] With the notable exception of the fief descending from Blohin [*sic*] in 1086 to the Bloyou family for 250 years.

[9] Earl Reginald's comital fief can be inferred from later records.

earliest and in some respects the most illuminating.[10] In it we meet for the first time some of those new tenants and new fiefs to which reference has been made. The text of the charter printed by Round, and checked against the manuscript by Richard Sharpe, is as follows:

> Isti sunt homines qui fuerunt [presentes] ubi Henricus rex concessit Bernardo scriptori et heredibus suis et cartis suis confirmavit omnes terras quas habuit Bernardus in Cornubia de eo et dominis suis, scilicet totam terram que fuit Gisulfi et omnes res suas, et terram que fuit Theodulfi avi Bernardi et Brictrici avunculi sui et Ailsii patris sui, et totam terram que fuit Dodonis et terram que fuit Rann[ulfi] Cancellarii in castello, et ecclesiam de Lanwittonia, et terram de Trecharl et de Menwinnoc et Cheulent de feudo episcopi, et terram de Charnbrixi de feoudo[11] Ricardi de Luci, et terram de Trethu de feudo Willelmi filii Ricardi, et terram de Treghestoc de feudo Rogeri de Curcell[is], et terram de Botwei de Wigan' de feudo Ricardi de Luci, et ecclesiam de Lischaret de feudo Reg[is], et wirgultum castelli de feudo Rualdi filii Wigani, et terram de Treualrig de feudo Andree de Vitreio, scilicet Rogerus episcopus Saresberiensis et Rannulfus cancellarius et Gaufridus capellanus suus et Robertus de Sigillo et Nigellus de Albin[eio] et Gaufridus de Glintton' et Edwardus Sar[esberiensis] et Willelmus de Sancto Claro et Grimbaldus medicus.[12]

In the commentary which now follows I have numbered Bernard's possessions according to their sequence in the foregoing charter.

1. Four tenements described as *in castello*[13] are here confirmed by the king to Bernard, namely that which had previously been held by Gisulf (a scribe—see Round, *op. cit.*, p. 422), secondly that which had been held, presumably consecutively, by Bernard's grandfather, uncle and father,[14] thirdly that which a certain Dodo had held, and fourthly that which Ranulf the chancellor had held. In 1123 this castle can only have been Dunheved castle, later called Launceston castle,[15] which was then in the king's hand. It had

---

[10] The invaluable Pipe Roll of 1130 contains but little specifically *feudal* information about Cornwall.
[11] *Sic.*
[12] Round, 'Bernard, the king's scribe', p. 418.
[13] *In castello* and *in feudo episcopi* evidently refer to their respective four preceding tenements.
[14] Hull and Sharpe, 'Peter of Cornwall' (see next note), p. 47.
[15] Its name, *Lanstavan-ton, followed the priory upon its removal from St Stephen by Launceston in c.1154-5 to a site across the valley under Dunheved castle. (But see P. L. Hull and R. Sharpe, 'Peter of Cornwall and Launceston', *Cornish Studies*, 13 (1986), 5-53, at pp. 37-8.)

been built, it appears, by Count Robert of Mortain after the Norman Conquest to be his military capital of Cornwall;[16] and such it continued to be for subsequent earls and dukes of Cornwall. At the date of this charter the only other feudal castles in the county would probably have been Norman motte and bailey constructions at Old Cardinham, Trematon and Restormel,[17] where the barons of Cardinan, Trematon and Bodardel had their respective strongholds. The existence of these four tenements within the bailey of Dunheved castle as well as of another tenement mentioned in a different memorandum in this series printed by Round is agreeable with recently found archaeological evidence that foundations of this period underlie others of buildings erected within and near the wall of the bailey in the 13th century.[18]

2. The Church of *Lanwittonia*. This entry is the first of four in the charter concerning possessions of Bernard within the ancient episcopal manor of Lawhitton which comprised the parishes (as they eventually became) of Lawhitton, South Petherwin, Trewen and Lezant. By the year 1123 this church of Lawhitton may hardly yet have become a parish church: being sited among the demesnes of the bishop's manor[19] it may have been a manorial foundation of the 11th century rather than the successor of a Celtic foundation on the site. As Ann Preston-Jones and Oliver Padel have pointed out, the earlier manorial capital must have been at the place in the parish of South Petherwin called Oldwit *(Yolde Lawhitta* in a rental of the manor in 1538).[20] Perhaps the capital of the manor was removed to the present Lawhitton, more distant from Dunheved castle, when Count Robert of Mortain appropriated part of the episcopal manor for the construction of that castle and the enclosure of its park.

---

[16] According to archaeological and historical evidences. In 1478 William of Worcester called it the *Castrum de Morteyn alias Lancestdon in Lancestdon: The Itineraries of William Worcestre*, ed. J. H. Harvey (Oxford, 1969), p. 84.

[17] C. A. Ralegh Radford found Norman foundations of the Gate Tower *(Restormel Castle*, Min. of Works publication, London, 1947).

[18] Round, 'Bernard, the king's scribe', p. 420. This interesting abstract mentions land inside the castle 'between the well and the chapel' given to Bernard for his accommodation. Mr. Andrew Saunders, Chief Inspector of Ancient Monuments, informed me (letter, 3 December 1983) that no chapel site had been unearthed, though some wells had been, during recent excavations in the bailey of Launceston castle.

[19] DRO, 382/134106. Also Tithe Apportionment of Lawhitton parish.

[20] DRO, *ibid.*

3. *Trecharl* (i.e. Trekarl or Trecarl: as in Domesday Book so also in this charter Cornish place-names containing the letters 'k' and hard 'c' are spelt with the letters 'ch' instead. Other examples will be found below in the sections numbered 5, 6 and 10). Trekarl is now Trecarrel in the parish of Lezant. It became the residence of Bernard's younger brother, Jordan of Trekarl,[21] whose posterity long continued there.

4. *Menwinnoc* is Menwenick in the parish of Trewen.

5. *Cheulent* (i.e. Keulent, as explained under no. 3 above) has now become Trekelland in Lezant parish, but erroneously. Its prefix 'Tre-' is an unwarranted 19th-century addition to its name. During the 18th century the name was usually Kelland, sometimes Calland, in manorial records.[22] A rental of the manor in 1538 gives it as *Kewelond*, which makes the identity with Keulent *(Cheulent)* very apparent.[23] Yet even in the 19th century the correct form of the name persisted as late as 1845, when the tenement was called Kelland.[24] In the Tithe Apportionment of Lezant parish in 1840 the tenement is indeed miscalled *Trekelland;* but two of its fields retained the older form in their name *Kelland Hill*. Trekelland in Lezant parish should not be confused with the place-name Trekelland in the neighbouring parish of Lewannick, whose earlier forms are quite different, viz. *Trekellearn* 1748, *Trekellerne* 1710, and *Trekeleren* 1616.[25] All Lewannick parish lay outside the episcopal manor of Lawhitton.

6. *Charnbrixi* (i.e. Karnbrixi or Carnbrixi, as explained under no. 3 above). In another document of this series printed by Round a certain Brichtnot, Latinized as *Brichtnotus*, quitclaimed to Bernard his right in one acre of land and his houses in *Canbrixi*, which is evidently a miscopying of the word Carnbrixi.[26]

Though the word 'carn' is a common element of place-names in the west of Cornwall it is much rarer in the east where Bernard's Cornish possessions were. There is, however, in the eastern parish of Altarnun, a distinctive hill called Carn or Carne which gave its name to the three medieval settlements of

---

[21] See Hull and Sharpe, 'Peter of Cornwall', pp. 49-50.
[22] DRO, 382/9157, and 382/97697½ [*sic*].
[23] DRO, 382/134106, fo. 53.
[24] RIC, PE, bundle 9/25.
[25] *Seriatim*—Martin's map 1748; RIC, Henderson, calendar 9, Survey of Trelosk manor, 1710; PRO, Wards 7/58/198.
[26] Round, 'Bernard, the king's scribe', p. 420.

East Carn, West Carn and South Carn. Of these three, South Carn or South Carne became the titular capital of a small eclectic manor assembled, in or before the 14th century, by members of the Trelawny family. There formerly existed at Trelawne in Pelynt parish, where this family subsequently settled, a register of its title-deeds of estates which was compiled by Edward Trelawny in 1593. In it he recorded the acquisition some three years previously (in Anno 32 Elizabeth) by Jonathan Trelawny from Christopher Govett, junior, of 'South Caron Bisky alias South Caron Biskey Parke'.[27] In that part of Cornwall 'park' meant an ordinary field, though in moorland regions like Altarnun it might be an extensive one. The spelling *South Caron* for South Carn was prevalent in its manorial records of that time, but the older and better spelling, South Carne, was subsequently restored. This place-name in the register recurs in a document dated 1695 as 'South Carne alias Carne Biskey'.[28]

No other known place-name in Devon or Cornwall—Bernard had possessions in both—at all resembles the name Carnbrixi; but here the resemblance, even after the lapse of some five centuries, is so close as to justify, *prima facie*, the identification of Carnbrixi with Carne Biskey (to use the spelling of 1695). This identification is strongly supported by tenurial similarities common to both. Bernard, as this charter states, held Carnbrixi *(Charnbrixi)* 'of the fief of Richard de Luci'. The Trelawnys held their manor of South Carne, which included Carne Biskey, in socage of the manor of *Treglastan*, now Treglasta,[29] which is shown by records to have been a demesne manor belonging in 1194 to a grandchild[30] of another Richard de Luci, no less a person than the great Justiciar of King Henry II. Round has pointed out that the Justiciar must have been of a later generation than the Richard de Luci of this charter.[31] Perhaps they were father and son, but they must anyway have been closely related because (as will be shown) the Justiciar's lands in Cornwall are found to have included both the fiefs belonging to the earlier Richard de Luci of which Bernard held, respectively, his tenements of Carnbrixi

---

[27] This Register was destroyed at Exeter by enemy action in 1942. But Charles Henderson's transcript of it is at Truro, RIC, Henderson, Calendar 23, under the 'Manor of South Carn'.

[28] Marriage settlement, John Morth with Elizabeth Buller, 1695, seen by the author at Morval House in 1939, now removed.

[29] PRO, Inquisition post mortem of Jonathan Trelawnye, kt, in 1604.

[30] Whose Cornish demesne manors, including *Treglastan*, being in the king's hand, were accounted for in the Pipe Roll of 1194 (PRS, n.s., vol. 5. p. 21).

[31] Round, 'Bernard, the king's scribe', p. 419.

and Botwei. This raises the possibility that not only these two fiefs but also others of the Justiciar's extensive and scattered Cornish manors and fees were inherited from the same man.[32]

The charter does not indeed state that Carnbrixi was held by Bernard of a manor called *Treglastan* and that the earlier Richard held the latter. But Bernard's successors in title did so, and *Treglastan* was one of the Justiciar's demesne manors inherited by his descendants. Moreover *Treglastan* manor included much of the later parishes of Davidstow and Altarnun, with South Carne and Carne Biskey in the latter.

A matter of some interest is raised by the personal name, Brichtnot, of the man who had rights in Carnbrixi to quitclaim to Bernard, as already mentioned. The name Carnbrixi means Brixi's Hill or Tor and its element 'brixi' represents OE *Beorhtsige*. So it is a suggestive coincidence that Brichtnot's own name, from OE *Beorhtnoth*, includes that element *beorht* which, in origin, Carnbrixi also contained. There is thus a possibility that this Brichtnot was a descendant at no great remove of the man, Brixi (*Beorhtsige*), who gave his name to this 'carn'. In OE family nomenclature one element of a man's name was frequently included in the name of his son or grandson, as perhaps *beorht* was here included in the names Brixi and Brichtnot. But it must be admitted that *beorht* was so frequent in OE personal names that this interesting conjecture is very speculative indeed.

7. *Trethu* 'of the fief of William son of Richard'. The place must be Trethew, a small manor in Menheniot parish at its junction with Morval parish. The manor was a member of the barony and honour of Cardinan (Cardinham in the parish of that name) and is so described in feudal records. By 1123 the Domesday Book baron, Richard son of Turold, was evidently dead for this is his son, William son of Richard, the second baron. When the demesnes and fees of the barony were dispersed by the heiress, Isolda de Cardinan, about the year 1267, the manor of Cardinan with the fee of the manor of Trethew passed to the Devonshire family of Dinham or Dynham. A survey of the Dynham inheritance made in 1566 contains, under the heading 'Fees of Cardinham', an entry saying that the heirs of Lord Broke hold by knight's

---

[32] The Justiciar's Cornish estates can be ascertained from the known heritage of his descendants.

service *Trethewe next Liscard,* doing therefor suit of court [to Cardinham manor] and paying for a fine of suit twelvepence.[33] At an earlier period, in 1332, the service due had been for one knight's fee.[34]

8. *Treghestoc* 'of the fief of Roger de Curcell[is]' is now Tregastick in Morval parish, contiguous with Trethew in Menheniot. About the year 1250 Randulf, lord of *Trethu,* gave to his sister and her husband in marriage his land of *Tregeustoc,* described as being an acre of land in the fee of *Fawyton.*[35] The manor of *Fawyton,* named from Fawton in the parish of St Neot, was of great importance in the 11th century when it was held in demesne by Count Robert of Mortain himself.[36] After the forfeiture of his son's lands this manor escheated to King Henry I and by him must have been given to this Roger de Curcellis. By 1149 it had passed to Wandregesil de Curcellis.[37] Their name was taken from Courseulles in Calvados, as also the name of the Domesday Book baron in Somersetshire, Roger *de Curcella,* is believed to have been.

9. Wigan's land of *Botwei* 'of the fief of Richard de Luci'. This is no doubt Bodway, in Menheniot parish, near Trethew manor but, unlike Trethew, a member of the manor of *Tregrilla,* now Tregrill, in that parish.[38] Here is further evidence that estates of this Richard de Luci descended to Richard de Luci the Justiciar (see under no. 6 above). Tregrilla manor was held in free socage of the manor of Boconnoc, in Boconnoc parish,[39] which was held, in its turn, by knight's service of the manor and honour of Lantyan in the parish of St Samson, near Fowey in Cornwall.[40] Lantyan manor had been another, perhaps the most valuable, demesne manor in Cornwall of the Justiciar.[41] It was retained as a demesne manor by his various successors in title for centuries after his other Cornish manors no longer were.[42]

[33] DRO, Book Quarto 009. 04, fo. 87.
[34] *Cal. Inquisitions post mortem,* vol. VII, no. 462.
[35] CRO, WM/170.
[36] Exon.DB, p. 207, *Fauuitone.*
[37] *Launceston Cartulary,* no. 81.
[38] Brit. Lib., Add. Charters 64453.
[39] Charter of 1437 (in the author's collection). [Now in the RIC, Truro. O.J.P.]
[40] The earliest statement, A.D.1211-12, is in the *Red Book of the Exchequer,* ed. H. Hall, vol. II (London, 1896), p. 612. Later rentals of the honour and manor of Lantyan are among Rashleigh MSS in the CRO.
[41] See note 30.
[42] Lantyan manor was owned successively by Lucy, Rivers, Monthermer, and Montague, earls of Salisbury. In the 16th century it was purchased by Rashleigh of Cornwall.

10. The church of *Lischaret* [i.e. Liskaret, now Liskeard] 'of the king's fief'. Liskeard manor was another which had been a demesne manor of Count Robert.[43] Bernard would have received its church by favour of King Henry I whose scribe he was. Subsequently the manor of Liskeard passed to Reginald, Earl of Cornwall, that king's illegitimate but privileged son, who gave the church to the monks of Launceston Priory.[44] With the church went its valuable glebe, increasingly to be built over by the expanding new borough of Liskeard. This glebe the Austin Canons of Launceston Priory called their manor of Hagland.[45] The name may be derived from OE *Halig-land,* 'holy land', because holy land or glebe of the church is precisely what Hagland manor was.

11. *A virgate* [of land] *of the castle* 'of the fief of Ruald son of Wigan'. We may be back at Dunheved castle for there is no reason to suppose (in the absence of archaeological investigations) that Liskeard castle had been built as early as 1123: if it had been, it would have been of the king's fief, like Liskeard church. Perhaps it is straining the meaning of these few words, but it may be significant that the phrase used here to describe the location of this land is *wirgultum castelli,* 'a virgate of the castle', and not the phrase previously used in this charter, namely *in castello,* 'in the castle' (i.e. inside its bailey). If the distinction between the two phrases was deliberate it may mean that this virgate belonged to the castle but lay where a settlement of traders and castle employees was establishing the beginnings of the later town of Launceston, outside the bailey. Whether at this date such a suburb of the castle was enclosed by a defensive rampart, which might perhaps be thought of as an outer ward, is something we must leave to archaeologists to tell us in due course. There is reason to think that Ruald son of Wigan was an Angevin:[46] he was a considerable landowner in the counties of Cornwall, Devonshire, Suffolk and Cambridgeshire in 1130.[47] Another charter in this series which Round printed concerns a grant made to Bernard by this Ruald of churches formerly belonging to a certain Brictric *Walensis*.[48] But it is not very likely that he is to be identified

---

[43] Exon.DB, p. 207, *Liscarret.*
[44] *Launceston Cartulary,* no. 493.
[45] At first *Halgelond, Launceston Cartulary,* no. 509.
[46] *Recte* Wingand. See note 50.
[47] *Magnum Rotulum Scaccarii,* ed. J. Hunter (London, 1833).
[48] Round, 'Bernard, the king's scribe', pp. 419-20.

with that Bristric who had held the manor of Dodbrook in Devonshire before, but not after, the Norman Conquest;[49] though Dodbrook manor was one of those which Ruald came to hold in the 12th century.

Ruald son of Wigand had two sons, Alfred and Hamo. He and they were alive in or shortly after 1136.[50] The Devonshire family styled Fitz Roald was descended from Alfred.

12. *Treualrig* 'of the fief of Andrew de Vitreio' must be the place which was called Trevarledge in 1841. It was in the parish of Advent and was called *Treualrigg* in 1337 when it was a member of the manor of Helstone in Trigg, in northern Cornwall.[51] Andrew's family, named from Vitré in Brittany, continued to be landowners or custodians for the king of escheated estates in Cornwall until the 13th century. During John's reign another Andrew *de Viteri* was given lands in Cornwall by the king who, however, afterwards deprived him of them.[52] Among manors which this later Andrew had held in Cornwall was this very manor of Helstone in Trigg[53] (the more valuable manor of Helston in Kerrier, a demesne manor of the earldom of Cornwall, continued to be in the king's possession at that time); but by 1227 this manor of *Helleston* (in Trigg) had passed to Theodoric *Teutonicus, alias* Tyes, whose family was favoured by King Henry III. Thus it chanced that the manor of Helstone in Trigg found a niche in English history because it was one of the eight manors in Cornwall for the control of which the new-made earl of Cornwall, Richard, disputed with his brother, King Henry III, to the verge of civil war in 1227.[54]

It is interesting to find an Andrew *de Vitreio* holding the manor of Helstone in Trigg before 1123 (as he must have done to be overlord of its tenement of

---

[49] Exon.DB, p. 452, *Dodebroca*.

[50] H. R. Watkin, *History of Totnes ...*, vol. II (Torquay, 1917), Plate III, Totnes Priory deed XIV.

[51] DCRS, n. s. 17, p. 13 (*Caption of Seisin of the Duchy of Cornwall*, 1337, ed. P. Hull).

[52] *Rotuli Litterarum Clausarum*, vol. I, ed. T. D. Hardy (RC, 1833) p. 407. Lands of this or an earlier Andrew de Veteri were in the king's hand in 1197 (see PRS, 8, p. 3).

[53] In a wildly anachronistic list made in 1302 (Just.1/117, m. 64) of tenants *in milicia* of the earl of Cornwall, Andrew *de Wytery* is shown as holding *Hebeston* (*recte Heleston* in Trigg). He did not in 1302, and this must be one of the entries relating to tenures early in the 13th century.

[54] The eight manors were *Alverton* (Madron parish), *Tybbestein* (Tybesta in Creed), *Braynel* (Brannel in St Stephen in Brannel), *Helleston* (Helstone in Trigg), *Penmayne* (in St Minver), *Tamerton* (North Tamerton), *Moreis* (Moresk in St Clement's), and *Rellinton* (Rillaton in Linkinhorne)—*Rotuli Litterarum Clausarum*, vol. II (ed. T. D. Hardy, 1844), p. 191.

Treualrig) and another man of the same name holding it early in the 13th century. But I do not know of any evidence that persons of their family had been holding it throughout the intervening years.

As has been said, the constitutional importance of this charter of King Henry I to Bernard his scribe lies in the glimpse it affords us of that king's dispositions of Count William's and some of his tenants' forfeited Cornish estates. We learn the names of three of the more important new landlords—men of the families of *de Luci*, *de Curcellis* and *de Vitreio*—as well as of lesser tenants whose impact upon the structure of feudal Cornwall was transitory.

6
Trezance, Lahays and the Manor of Cardinham

Devon and Cornwall Notes and Queries, 26 (1954-5), 203-8

CARDINHAM, JUST EASTWARD OF BODMIN, is today a lonely and beautiful parish rising in a tangle of sudden valleys from the wooded banks of the river Fowey into the long expanses of Foweymoor. In the early Middle Ages Cardinham had a special claim to distinction: it contained the seat of the most powerful baron in Cornwall. The earl of Cornwall, his overlord, was of course greater than he: but the earls were figures of national importance and can rarely have resided in their county. With the acquisition of the barony of Bodardel the lords of *Cardinan* held no less than 71 knight's fees of the combined baronies, scattered throughout Cornwall. The Honour of *Cardinan*, as it came to be called, seems to have come into existence after the Norman Conquest. Its first known holder, Richard fitz Turold, possessed it at the time of the Domesday Survey in 1086, and may have come from Normandy[1] in the train of Count Robert of Mortain to whom William the Conqueror, his half-brother, gave the county of Cornwall.

But in Domesday Book the name *Cardinan* is not mentioned: instead there stands at the head of the list of Richard's Cornish manors one with the name *Thersent*.[2] To Charles Henderson belongs the credit of perceiving that this

---

[1] It has been suggested that he was a member of the well-known family of Dinan, of Dinan and Dol in Brittany and afterwards of Devon. The suggestion rests solely on the similarity of the names Dinan and Cardinan and is not supported by anything else. The family at Cardinham described themselves as 'of Cardinan', and never used the name Dinan. Indeed their only discoverable connection with the Continent was not with either Normandy or Brittany but with Anjou. That, however, was in consequence of the gift of Tywardreath monastery, perhaps by William fitz Richard, to the abbey of St Serge at Angers in Anjou. It does not follow that the donor was necessarily an Angevin. Because of this donation the obits of William fitz Richard's mother, wife and daughter-in-law were observed at St Serge's Abbey (see Oliver's *Monasticon Exoniense*, p. 37 *et seq.* for the connection with St Serge's Abbey, and the Necrology of that abbey in the Municipal Library of Angers, MS. 837 (753), for the obits).

[2] Exeter Domesday, fol. 228b: printed in the Record Commissioners' *Domesday Book*, vol. IV, p. 207.

must be the place in Cardinham parish now called Trezance. Trezance lies high on a hillside; and Richard fitz Turold, or more probably his son, William fitz Richard, moved to a better site at *Cardinan*,[3] which became the name of the manor. The plan of his new castle[4] there, now called Old Cardinham, can easily be traced on a dominating spur of land above the narrow but precipitous valley under Cardinham church. That became the capital of the Honour of Cardinham, and there, no doubt, the courts baron of the manor were held. But in the process of time it became the practice to hold certain of the courts, namely the two annual law-courts with the court of the Fee of Cardinham, at a place more readily accessible to tenants journeying from distant regions. In 1566, and long previously, these courts were held at *Gretediche*.[5] This name is no longer remembered, but the site was the nearest piece of the manor (and, incidentally, of the parish) to the town of Bodmin, upon what was then unenclosed moorland. It was conveniently situated at the parish boundary alongside, and just south of, the old road from Bodmin to Temple (at this point now part of the A30 highway) where the Calliwith turnpike gate was afterwards erected; and it took its name from a great ditch which divided this piece of Cardinham manor moors from the priory of Bodmin's fields of Calliwith. This ditch, with the remains of a bank upon its northern side, was levelled by a 'bulldozer' some three years ago.[6] At the point where the junction of the ditch with the Bodmin-Cardinham parish boundary formed a corner of the Calliwith field called Ditch Park there stood, and still stands, a stone boundary cross. It no longer marks the apex of two meeting hedges on an open moor, because the moor has been enclosed, the hedges extended and new ones constructed. So it now appears to stand against a hedge inside a field: but in fact it must be close to, if not actually on, its original site. In 1613

---

[3] *Cardinan* may have been the name of an older, perhaps prehistoric, fort on the site of the medieval castle of *Cardinan*. The commanding position of the site makes it quite likely (but see note 22 below).

[4] It may have been one of the 'adulterine' castles erected in King Stephen's reign (the baron of *Cardinan* and his son-in-law the earl of Cornwall were deeply involved in the civil war). The mounds marking the bailey and motte are remarkably prominent; and the whole impressive site cries out for careful excavation.

[5] Survey of Cardinham manor: Exeter City Library, Quarto book, 009.04, fol. 75 *et seq.*

[6] Information from Mr. A. Dingle of Calliwith, aged 80 or more, farmer there for 50 years, formerly of Benorth in Cardinham.

it was called *Greedetch Cross*,[7] but since then it has usually been called Calliwith Cross[8]—a well-known bound-mark of Bodmin parish.

Fifty years ago there was an interesting tradition among old inhabitants that 'religious meetings' used to be held[6] on the same piece of land, now of course a field, that the Cardinham courts occupied (though of the courts themselves there seems no distinct memory). There may be in this tradition some dim recollection of the Wesleyan revival of the 18th century: in any case it testifies to the memory of a meeting-place there, religious or secular.

Before the move to Old Cardinham the capital of the manor was, as we have seen, at Trezance, a place divided for centuries into the interlocked farms of Higher and 'Lower Trezance' *(Over* and *Nether Tresans*[9] in 1566)—a name which at once suggests a derivation from the Cornish *tre(v)-sans*, holy farmstead. Although this may indeed be the correct explanation of the name the requisite early spellings are not yet forthcoming to substantiate it, and there is some evidence against it. In defiance of the official name 'Lower Trezance' the name of this farm has been changed to Teason—a process completed and accepted by the Ordnance surveyors within the past hundred years. The name Teason evidently represents a persistent vernacular version of the name Trezance (a 'Teason Meadow' belonged to this farm in 1839, though the farm itself was still called Lower Trezance[9]): that it is likely to be a really ancient traditional form of the name is proved by the name of a local inhabitant in 1421, Isabella Tersen,[10] and by the important spelling *Thersent*[2] in 1086. Teason, or *Tersen*, if the true form, would come from the Cornish *tyr - sans*, holy ground. On the face of it a change by metathesis from the much rarer *tyr* (or its form *ter*) to the extremely common *tre* is far more probable than the opposite change.[23] The argument, fortunately, is of no great consequence because both *Tre-sans* and *Ter-sans* agree in describing a place that had holy associations. In Cornwall that can only mean an association with one or more of those early Celtic missionaries or religious leaders commonly called the Cornish Saints. That this was so at Trezance we have the independent evidence of the presence

---

[7] Terrier of Cardinham parish, 1613; cited by C. G. Henderson.

[8] *Callywith Cross* in 1700; see Maclean's 'Trigg Minor', vol. I, p. 339.

[9] Tithe Apportionment of Cardinham parish, 1839, at the Tithe Redemption Commissioners' Office, London.

[10] *Cornwall Feet of Fines*, DCRS, vol. II (1950), no. 945.

there of a once celebrated holy-well, with the site of what must have been a fine well-chapel beside it. From this holy-well it was formerly the custom to draw the water for baptisms in the parish church;[11] and this link with Cardinham church points very strongly to St Meubred, patron saint of the church, as the patron also of the now saintless holy-well and chapel. Very little of St Meubred's legend has survived to our day though he must have had a considerable local cult in the Middle Ages, for he was known at Fowey in 1478, and was depicted in the new glass[12] (which can still be seen) of a window of St Neot's church in 1530. We can hardly reject the probability that his fame and his sanctity caused the name 'Holy Ground' to be given to the land around his spring, and, by implication, around his residence (one does not live far from one's drinking-water). Evidently, then, when the first Norman baron of *Cardinan* ruled his estates from Trezance he was holding secular court in a place already long venerated by the populace for religious reasons.

Perhaps it was the religious associations of Trezance that led one of the lords of *Cardinan* to restore a part of it to religious uses. One of these lords, before 1170,[13] had endowed and delivered to the care of the monks of Tywardreath monastery a small chapel and cell of monks called St Mary of the Vale at a place still called Lady Vale a mile downstream from his castle at Old Cardinham. About the year 1180 Robert fitz Robert,[14] great-grandson of Richard fitz Turold, added to this endowment at Lady Vale two other small properties in his manor of *Cardinan lebiri*, namely his manor mill of *Cardinan*, and an acre of land called *Leslof*.[15] These three small tenements the Black Monks of Tywardreath annexed to their nearest manor, *Grediowe* (Gready in Lanlivery), and administered thus until the Dissolution. Falling then into the king's hands the manor of Gready was by Henry VIII given to his Duchy of

---

[11] *Ancient and Holy Wells of Cornwall* by M. and L. Quiller Couch, p. 24.
[12] With the inscription *Sancte Meberede ora pro nobis*.
[13] The church of *Sancte Marie de Valle* was among the endowments confirmed to Tywardreath priory by Thomas, Archbishop of Canterbury, who was murdered in 1170; see Oliver's *Monasticon Exon.*, p. 41.
[14] There were only two barons of *Cardinan* who could have been styled *Robertus filius Roberti*. This must be the earlier of them because one of his witnesses was *Ricardus dapifer*. This Richard had been *dapifer*, or steward, of a still earlier baron, after whose death Richard soon ceased to attest charters.
[15] A photograph of this charter from the Wardour Castle muniments is reproduced in Yeatman's *History of the House of Arundel* as number 23 of the photographic appendix.

Cornwall. The manor was surveyed, with other royal estates, by the Parliamentarians in 1650, when it was found that there were still attached to the manor of *Gredioe* three isolated little tenements in Cardinham parish, namely *Ladie Vale alias Lady Vale* with 5 acres of land, *Cardinham Mills* with 2 acres, and *Le Hay* with 28 acres.[16] These three remained Duchy property until their sale in the present century. This continuous history of the three places makes certain, what otherwise might be doubtful, that *Le Hay* of 1650 is the same tenement as *Leslof* of *c*.1180. The name is now pronounced Layhays[6] (and was written so in 1839,[9] although the misleading spelling Lahays has since prevailed). Unfortunately the name *Leslof* cannot so far be interpreted with confidence. There are several possibilities, of which perhaps the most seductive supposes a derivation from the Cornish words *les*, breadth of land, and *lok*, religious cell, reviving memories of St Meubred and *Ter-sans,* Holy Ground (though *lok* occurs excessively rarely in Cornish place-names—Luxulyan may be the only example). Mr. R. Morton Nance thinks this derivation is a possibility. More prosaic would be a derivation of the second element of *Leslof* from the English word *loc(a)*, an enclosure, taking the first element *les* to be merely a form of the French definite article 'the' (which at that date, and for many centuries afterwards, was very commonly prefixed to place-names or field-names in Cornwall).[17] The strength of this theory lies in the fact that the subsequent name of this tenement actually was 'The Enclosure', *Le Hay* (French article and all); so that it is only necessary to postulate the substitution of one English word meaning 'enclosure' for another—the commoner word *hay* for the word *loc*.

Lahays, alias *Leslof,* is a small farm close to Trezance holy-well, compactly joined with the fields of Lower Trezance, alias Teason. Curiously enough Lahays and Lower Trezance are, after eight centuries, reunited in one ownership, and are now being farmed as one farm. The western boundary of

---

[16] PRO, E.317/Cornwall/16 [compare N. J. G. Pounds, *The Parliamentary Survey of the Duchy of Cornwall*, 2 vols., DCRS, n.s., 25 and 27 (1982-4), I, 42-3]. It was called *the hay* in 1566 and *Hays* in 1748 and 1813. A Cornish acre of 1180 might well be expressed as 28 English ones in 1650; in 1839 the figure was 38¾ acres.

[17] It actually occurs in the name *lebiri* in the very charter that names *Leslof* (see note 15 above): and it occurs, in the form *lez*, in a *Tresans* field-name in the survey of 1566 and frequently in other parts of that manuscript. Note also the modern vernacular pronunciation of the older *Le Hay* as *Lay*-hays, the accent being on the second syllable.

Lahays for many years must have been the open moor: the name of the next farm in that direction is Haygrove, indicating a later creation than Lahays, as also does the name of one of Haygrove's fields, Gunnivus in 1839,[9] which may contain the Cornish word *goon* or *gun*, meaning unenclosed land (the opposite of the English word *hay*).

Another interesting name is Place Green. In 1839 this was the name of two fields,[9] divided from Lahays by a road: but it must once have been an open space against the moor which lapped the higher side of Lahays. It probably included a curious patch of waste beside the road at this point. On the other hand, a neighbouring field in Lahays itself, called 'Place Green Field' in 1839,[9] seems to have borrowed its name from the company it kept.[18] 'The Green' is a common field-name in these parts for a meadow near a farmhouse—Trezance has one yet: the name means what it does in 'Village Green'. 'Place', however, is an uncommon name in Cornwall. It occurs in the parishes of Fowey, Padstow and St Anthony in Roseland as the name of the former court-house or administrative centre of monastic property—in these instances property of the monasteries of Tywardreath, Bodmin and Plympton, respectively—and must be derived in these cases from the French word *place*. What looks like the same name, but is quite different, is found at Place in Rame parish, an early record of which shows that the name in the 13th century was *La Pleistowie* (note the French definite article), a word clearly derived from the English *plegstow*, playground (cf. Plaistow in Derbyshire, Devonshire, Kent and Sussex). It is, in fact, analogous to the name 'Playing Place' found in mid-Cornwall, itself a translation of the Cornish *Plen-an-gwary*, a theatre where plays were performed. Place Green in Cardinham must belong to this latter class of, so to speak, place-names; there is nothing to indicate that it was ever even a separate tenement let alone an administrative centre, and it certainly was not monastic property. It is improbable that Place Green ever had a circular rampart like the typical Cornish playing-places: nothing of the sort is visible, and the use of the word 'green' indicates a different kind of arena and one that could be used as a sports-ground. On the assumption that the oldest form of the name was *plegstow* an existence of many centuries is required to account for the change to the modern form. We can therefore reasonably

[18] Two fields in Lahays, this one and its neighbour, are now sometimes called 'Place Green': but that is not their name in the Tithe Apportionment of 1839.

assume that Place Green was something of a social centre for the medieval folk of the farms near Trezance.

We have now followed several strands in the web of Cardinham's history and found that they all lead back to the immediate vicinity of Trezance. Thus, the lords of *Cardinan*, before they kept their state in Old Cardinham castle, ruled from *Thersent*, which is Trezance: their tenants, in the Middle Ages, resorted for entertainment or recreation to Place Green, next Trezance: the monks of distant Tywardreath priory were linked by their chapel at Lady Vale to their isolated farm at Lahays, next Trezance: the medieval parishioners of Cardinham, attending at their parish church on the festival of its patron saint, would hear references to the legend of St Meubred; and their thoughts would turn to his renowned holy-well and chapel at Trezance: and, long centuries earlier, the native Cornishmen of that region heard, watched and finally revered[20] the Celtic missionary who ever after was remembered as their principal evangelist, so that their place of worship was called St Meubred's Church; whose spring of drinking water was held to be sanctified by his use of it; and about whose habitation the very land was called *tyr-sans,* holy ground.

To this already long history we can add another chapter, taking the story of this remarkable district back into yet more remote past. On the hill above Trezance stands the great prehistoric earthwork of Bury Castle, a fortress of paramount importance in the centuries before Christ.[21] And Robert fitz Robert, baron of *Cardinan,* himself bears us witness of its lasting prestige when, in his charter more than a thousand years later, he included its name in that of his medieval manor of *Cardinan le Biri.*[22]

---

[19] C. G. Henderson MSS in the Royal Institution of Cornwall at Truro, Calendar 25.

[20] They appear to have cut his head off first, according to his picture in St Neot's Church window.

[21] See the chapter on 'The Iron Age' in Hencken's *Archaeology of Cornwall and Scilly,* and especially the map on p. 131.

[22] It was written *lebiri,* as quoted above (see notes 15 and, for the use of the French definite article, 17). The choice of this double name for his manor by Robert fitz Robert raises the interesting possibility that *Cardinan* is the original name of *le Biri* itself, that is, of Bury Castle on the moor. This attractive speculation would certainly explain the conjunction of the two names in this charter: but it would leave unexplained the problem of why, in that case, the name Cardinham has clung so very persistently to the site of the 12th-century castle in the valley below the moor. It would be rash to reject the evidence of the settled practice of eight hundred years on the strength of this one, not very explicit, text.

[The charter of *c.*1180 discussed here is now in Cornwall Record Office, ART1/6. While cataloguing this collection in 1993-4, I observed in the text one word overlooked in the interpretation given above. The dispository clause actually reads: 'dedi ... in manerio meo de Cardinan Lebiri *et* acram unam in augmentum que vocatur Leslof'. The word overlooked was the crucial *et* after *Lebiri* (written with the abbreviation '7': see the reproduction in P. Yeatman, *The Early History of the House of Arundel*, plate 23). The difference that this makes is as follows: the main gift made to Tywardreath Priory by Robert was actually the place called *Lebiri*, doubtless at or near the modern Little and Higher Bury, below Bury Castle; therefore the words 'Cardinan Lebiri' do not belong closely together (but rather 'dedi ... in manerio meo de Cardinan, *Lebiri*'), and the combined phrase was not a name for the manor, as taken above; and, finally, the gift of the acre called *Leslof* was, like the manorial mill, additional to the main gift (making good sense of *in augmentum*). The implications of this word in the charter were agreed between us when I pointed them out; but this does not, of course, detract from the value of the other observations made above.

The land called *Lebiri* seems to have been lost to the priory, since it does not appear in later surveys. In fact, none of the Cardinham lands appears in the rental of the priory's manors compiled in 1520-1 (Cornwall Record Office, ART3/1-2), though some at least still belonged to the priory then. For the tenements of Lady Vale, Lahays and Cardinham mill in 1650, as mentioned above, see now N. J. G. Pounds, *The Parliamentary Survey of the Duchy of Cornwall*, 2 vols, Devon and Cornwall Record Society, n. s., 25 and 27 (1982-4), I, 42; and, for the manor of Cardinham in 1566, see now H. S. A. Fox and O. J. Padel, *The Cornish Lands of the Arundell Family of Lanherne, Fourteenth to Sixteenth Centuries*, Devon and Cornwall Record Society, n. s., 41 (1998), pp. 177-87 (p. 182, etc., for Great Ditch). O.J.P.]

---

[23] [p.52] While this article was in the press the author discovered strong support for this theory in the spelling of this place-name as *Tersant* in 1347 (PRO, Just.1/1430, m. 6).

7
A Misdated Cornish Tax Account in the Book of Fees

Cornish Studies, 10 (1983), pp.19-26

IT IS NOT QUITE ACCURATE to call this predominantly feudal product a 'tax account', but in a concise title it is convenient.[1] The document is one of two similar accounts, both printed in the *Book of Fees*, of payments made or owed (nearly all in Cornwall) by 13th-century tenants *in milicia*, at the rate of two marks (26s. 8d.) on the fee, or 16s. 8d. on the small fee of Mortain. The text of this account is anonymous, undated and unassigned; but Sir Henry Maxwell Lyte, editing the *Book of Fees*, inferred from names of persons whose payments it records that it dealt with the scutage of *Kery*. He therefore printed it under the editorial dates 'A.D. 1228-1229'; but he could find no more material of that scutage to keep it company in the *Book of Fees*, where it stands in isolation.[2]

In that respect it is very different from the other Cornish account to which reference has been made. That is one among a legion of accounts from divers counties, all dealing with the collection of the Aid voted by the magnates in 1235 and delivered into the Exchequer in two deposits, one at Michaelmas, 1235, the other at Easter, 1236. This latter Cornish account[3] was rendered (according to this printed text) by Henry of *Bodegrane* [read *Bodrygan*] and Simon of Brakel[ege], described in it as the *collectores auxilii comitatus Cornubie*.[4] They are known from Pipe and Close rolls to have collected the Aid of 1235 in the county of Cornwall.[5]

---

[1] In this article I am indebted to Dr. Paul Brand, of University College, Dublin [now of All Souls College, Oxford], for valuable suggestions and criticisms; also to Mr. Oliver Padel for editorial assistance.

[2] *The Book of Fees* (H.M. Stationery Office, London, 1920), I, pp. 393-4.

[3] *Ibid.*, pp. 435-7.

[4] *Ibid.*, p. 435.

[5] *Ibid.*, p. 437, note 2. *Close Rolls, Hen. III*, vol. 3 (1234-7), p. 190. See also S. K. Mitchell, *Studies in Taxation under John and Henry III* (New Haven, 1914), pp. 208-14.

Examination of the alleged scutage of *Kery* account, however, shows that Sir Henry was misled into making that attribution chiefly by a certain entry in it which states that William *Bruer* [William Briwere the younger] 'holds' ten fees in *Middelond*.[6] Briwere died in or shortly before February, 1233, so Sir Henry sought an earlier origin for the account.[7] Other factors indicated the scutage of *Kery* as the only possible *earlier* occasion.[8] It appears, however, that this crucial statement about Briwere's present tenure was anachronistic when it was first penned, for it is at variance with overwhelming internal evidence in its own document. For example, in that account Gervase of Tintagel was charged the levy on two fiefs, separately.[9] One of them, of five fees Mortain in *Hornicote*, was his patrimony. The other, consisting of one-twentieth of a fee in *Merthin', Winiainton'* and *Thamerton'* (Merthen, Winnianton and North Tamerton), he acquired by an exchange with Richard, Earl of Cornwall. The texts of Gervase's two charters in that business have been preserved. By the first he assured to Richard the castle of Tintagel and access to it through Gervase's own manor of Bossiney. This charter[10] can be dated to April or May 1233, by the names of its first five witnesses, *Willelmo de Raleg[e], Henrico de Tracy, Jordano Oliver, Willelmo de Insula, Adam filio Willelmi, tunc Justiciariis itinerantibus in Cornubia*—all of them experienced judges. This, in 1233, was the first general eyre to have been held in Cornwall for more than thirty years.[11] Its profits were probably granted by the king to his brother, Richard, Earl of Cornwall,[12] though its rolls have not survived and Earl Richard's administrative records have been lost.[13] Gervase's subsequent charter, by which he conveyed to Richard the manor of Bossiney itself in return for those three aforesaid manors (which he should hold of Richard by one-twentieth part of a fee), cannot be dated so precisely.[14] But the king's confirmation of Richard's alienation to Gervase of

---

[6] *Book of Fees*, I, p. 393: *Willelmus Bruer tenet in Middelond cum pertinenciis x. feoda. Pacavit vj.l. ix.s. viij.d.*
[7] *Ibid.*, p. 395.
[8] *Ibid.*, p. 393.
[9] See the abstract below.
[10] Cartulary of Earl Edmund, PRO E.36/57, no. 163.
[11] *Annales Theokesberie* (*Annales Monastici*, vol.I, 1864, ed. Luard [Rolls Series], p. 90).
[12] N. Denholm-Young, *Richard of Cornwall* (Oxford, 1947), p. 29, citing *Close Rolls*, p. 227.
[13] For the final concords from the 1233 eyre see *Cornwall Feet of Fines*, I (Devon & Cornwall Record Society, Exeter, 1912), nos. 257-68 (and, misdated, 269).
[14] PRO E.36/57, no. 57.

those three manors is dated 4 January 1236.[15] The exchange was probably effective in Cornwall some little time before that date; for Richard was impatient of royal tergiversations touching the lands of his Cornish earldom. The exchange was, in any event, effective in time for Gervase to be charged in this levy on his newly-acquired three manors. A document which knows of the acquisition by Gervase of one-twentieth part of a fee in those three manors cannot have been written during the lifetime of William Briwere the younger: but a document written in 1235 or 1236 could know of it, and might also copy from an unrevised feodary roll the statement that Briwere 'holds' the *Middelond* fees—as he did until his death early in 1233. Feodary rolls are prone to tenurial anachronisms.

The entry concerning Gervase's one-twentieth part of a fee is, in itself, decisive proof that its document cannot refer to the scutage of *Kery*, but must apply to some occasion after May, 1233. And when it is compared, item by item, with the authenticated[16] account of the Cornwall collection of the Aid of 1235 it becomes apparent that both accounts must have a common origin in a single collection. The proof of that lies in the financial particulars they contain and it is, I venture to think, incontrovertible. The full texts of both accounts can be consulted in the *Book of Fees*; but in order to facilitate comparison of their contents I print an abstract of them below (with christian names in English) having their corresponding entries juxtaposed.

Before I do that I ought, perhaps, to comment on the peculiar importance of the issue at stake, namely the correct dating of the alleged scutage of *Kery* account.

Loss of administrative records of the earldom of Cornwall, especially during the rule of Earl Richard from 1227 till 1272, often without equivalent matter appearing in Pipe rolls, has left Cornwall ill-supplied with datable feudal particulars during that period. Notices, for instance, of payments of scutage and reliefs would have been of great assistance in the task of dating contemporary Cornish charters by the names of their witnesses. In the absence of such sources of information these two, apparently securely dated, lists of Cornwall's most important landlords (possibly the only surviving and certainly the most readily accessible lists of Earl Richard's tenants by knight's service

---

[15] *Cal. Charter Rolls*, I, p. 215.

A Misdated Cornish Tax Account in the Book of Fees

holding of him as of his Cornish earldom) have been much relied upon by students when trying to date charters. Unfortunately, as J.H. Round has observed, 'There is ... no limit to the errors that may arise even from a single mistake' in dating historical documents.[17] If such an important feudal schedule as this impugned one gives false information about eminent landlords its misleading influence will be, and has been, incalculable.

In the following pages it will be convenient to refer to the authenticated Aid of 1235 account as 'Y' and to the unknown one, namely the alleged scutage of *Kery* account, as 'X'. The following are characteristic examples of the literary formulae employed in them (though with slight variations in Y).

> Y Iidem [*scil.* collectores] reddunt compotum de xvj.l . et xiiij.s. iiij.d. de xx. feodis Morton' honoris Matildis de Lucy et Roberti filii Walteri in Myneli et Lantyen. In thesauro xv.l. xij.d. Et debent xxxiij.s. et iiij.d.[18] [When payment was made in full by a tenant Y concludes his entry with the formula 'Et quietus est'.]
>
> X Robertus filius Walteri et Matildis de Luci tenent in Mineli et in Lantian xx. feoda. Pacaverunt xv.l. xij.d.[19]
>
> (*See pp. 64-6*)

It will be observed that, for all its brevity, X either states or implies as many particulars as Y does. In X the assessments and the residual debts after payments are not specified, as they are in Y; but, as the rate of the levy in X is known, those items can always be calculated from the number of fees and the amount paid to the accountants, both of which are given in X. One other characteristic of X should be noticed: it is concerned only with monies received, which explains its omission of some items appearing in Y (apparent exceptions to this characteristic will be discussed later).

In the analysis or abstract which now follows I have enclosed the unspecified but ascertainable amounts applying to X within (brackets). The sequence of entries followed here is that in Y, from which that in X differs only slightly. I have added numbers to the entries for reference.

---

[16] But in this copy not inerrant.
[17] *Cal. of Documents ... in France*, edit. J. H. Round (London, 1899), p. xviii.
[18] *Op. cit.*, I, 435.
[19] *Ibid.*, p. 393.

Y (but not X) concludes with a summary added in the Exchequer:

Summa tocius thesauri superioris allocati ciiij^{xx}v.l. x.s. x.d. [£185 10s. 10d.] quos recognoscunt se recepisse, de quibus in duabus talliis clx. et xix.l. xij.s. ix.d. [£160 and £19 12s. 9d.] Et debent cxviij.s. iij.ob. [£5 18s. 3½d][20]

The collectors, that is, acknowledge that they have received £185 10s. 10d., of which they have delivered in two tallies £179 12s. 9d., and still owe £5 18s. 3½d. of it. As is often the case with copied Roman numerals, error has crept in here: these figures are inconsistent. The two statements of what was collected—the total, and then its constituent amounts—disagree. Admittedly the discrepancy is only 2½d.; but it serves to warn us of this pervasive danger. Indeed, if anyone cares to reckon up, item by item, the monies received by the collectors (in the 'payment' column) according to this, the Y, account, their sum will be found to be £185 19s. 2½d., thus disagreeing yet again with the Exchequer totals. It is perhaps fortunate that some financial particulars in Y are patently inaccurate (see below), whereby this disagreeable total of the several items is vitiated to an unknown extent.

Taking Y and X together, 34 fiefs are mentioned, though not always by name: but from only 30 of them are corresponding receipts or defaults of payments entered in both Y and X. The four entries lacking these comparable particulars are the ones which I have numbered 25, 26, 32 and 34.

Of the 30 comparable payments in Y and X 18 are from fiefs whose assessments were paid in full. There is, perhaps, nothing very significant in any fief which paid in full on one occasion doing the same on another—supposing, with the editor, that Y and X refer to two different collections made at the same rate. But it is otherwise when we come to consider entries about corresponding fiefs in Y and X whose assessments (declared in Y, ascertainable in X) were only partly paid to the collectors. These partial payments follow no discoverable system: their amounts vary erratically and sometimes in strange, fractional proportions of their assessments. Yet, irregular or astonishing though these partial payments are, no less than 10 of them (out of the remaining comparable 12) agree exactly with their corresponding entries in Y and X. Moreover, the two remaining entries (2 and 28) prove to have no evidential value in this comparison because, as will be shown,

[20] *Ibid.*, p. 437.

self-contradictions in their figures in Y destroy the basis for a confident comparison of them with those in X.

Here, then, is a degree of concordance beyond any possibility of chance, as a glance at some examples of partial payments will quickly convince anyone. Both accounts, for instance, agree that:

£48	3s.	10d.	was paid instead of	£49	3s.	4d.	(no. 1);
£15	0s.	12d.	was paid instead of	£16	13s.	4d.	(no. 3);
£ 3	8s.	6½d.	was paid instead of	£ 4	3s.	4d.	(no. 12);
£ 1	7s.	10½d.	was paid instead of	£ 2	15s.	6d.	(no. 17);
£ 1	5s.	0d.	was paid instead of	£ 5	16s.	8d.	(no. 20).

I cannot think that this mounting series of sums of money coinciding in all thirty comparable entries, save in the two with dubious figures, can be explained satisfactorily by any other hypothesis than that both Y and X are accounts of a single collection, and that one is necessarily the collection of the Aid of 1235.

Having established by their financial evidence that Y and X are two versions of a single collection, made in 1235 or 1236, we may now examine errors or apparent contradictions occurring in other contents of Y and X. The error which has had the most serious consequence is, of course, the statement, discussed above, in X that William Briwere [the younger] was the present tenant of the fees of *Middelond*. The editor of the *Book of Fees* relied on this and was misled. But there is also in X another similar error, though it has not had the same unfortunate consequence. X states that Bartholomew son of *Thorold* paid the levy on his fief in Stratton, whereas Y makes it clear that Bartholomew *Toret* was already dead. As with the Briwere entry, this inaccuracy in X is likely to be due to reliance upon an unrevised feodary roll, though possibly a recent roll. Bartholomew was not the son of a man christened Thorold, but of one whose patronymic was Turet.

As has already been mentioned, the only two entries, numbers 2 and 28, in which there are disagreements between Y and X about payments received by the collectors are of uncertain value. In number 2 the difference between the figures given in Y and X only amounts to one shilling; but it cannot be corrected with certainty because the sum given in Y disagrees with the residual

[*continued on p. 67*]

ANALYSIS

Reference	Tenant	Fief	Fees	Assessment £ s d	Payment £ s d	Owing £ s d
1 Y	Reginald de Valle Torta	Tremeton	59	49 3 4	48 3 10	19 6
X	Reginald de Valle Torta		59	(49 3 4)	48 3 10	(19 6)
2 Y	Andrew de Cardinan	Cardinan & Botardel	71	59 3 4	58 11 8	12 4
X	A. de Cardinan		71	(59 3 4)	58 12 8	(10 8)
3 Y	Matilda de Lucy & Robert son of Walter	Myneli & Lantyen	20	16 13 4	15 0 12	1 12 4
X	Robert son of Walter & Matilda de Luci	Mineli & Lantian	20	(16 13 4)	15 0 12	(1 12 4)
4 Y	Herbert de Pinn & Walter son of William, of their wives' heritage					
X	William Bruer	Middelond	10	8 6 8	6 9 8	1 17 0
			10	(8 6 8)	6 9 8	(1 17 0)
5 Y	William de Botereus	Talcarn	12½	10 8 4	10 8 4	is quit
X	William de Boteraus	Thalcarn	12½	(10 8 4)	10 8 4	(nil)
6 Y	Radulf Blonyo	Polrede	7	6 3 4	4 2 6	2 0 10
X	Randulf Blowio	Polrode	7	(5 16 8)	4 2 6	(1 14 2)
7 Y	Simon Pincerne	Lanbo	½	8 4	8 4	is quit
X	Simon Pincerna	Lanbou	½	(8 4)	8 4	(nil)
8 Y	Richard Bordon	Penros	½	8 4	8 4	is quit
X	Richard Burdun	Penros	½	(8 4)	8 4	(nil)
9 Y	Henry de Heriz	Ebbeford	1	16 8	16 8	is quit
X	Henry de Heris	Hebbeford	1	(16 8)	16 8	(nil)
10 Y	Robert de Bikeleg's fee which Hugh de Boney holds of his wife's heritage	Hylton	5	4 3 4	4 3 4	is quit
X	Hugh de Boley	Hilton	5	(4 3 4)	(4 3 4)	(nil)
11 Y	Gilbert Anglicus	Wadevat	1	16 8	16 8	is quit
X	Gilbert Anglicus	Wadefat	1	(16 8)	16 8	(nil)
12 Y	Gervase de Tintagel	Hornicote & Tintagel	5	4 3 4	3 8 6	½ 14 9½
X	Gervase de Tinthagel	Hornicote	5	(4 3 3)	3 8 6½	14 9½

64

13 Y	Huward de Bykel[ege]	Treveris	½	8 4	8 4	is quit
X	Huward de Bykeley	Trefris	½	(8 4)	8 4	(nil)
14 Y	Henry son of William	Rerradoc	4	3 6 8	2 9 8	17 0
X	Henry son of William	Rerradoc	4	(3 6 8)	2 9 8	(17 0)
15 Y	Reginald *Walensis* & Henry *de Tredaec*	Tregamedon, Tredaec & Trelowyen	3	2 10 0	2 6 8	3 4
X	Reginald *Walensis* & Henry *de Tredaec*	Tregamedon, Tredaec & Treluyen	3	(2 10 0)	2 6 8	(3 4)
16 Y	William son of Richard	Plenint	1	16 8	16 8	is quit
X	William son of Richard	Plenint	1	(16 8)	16 8	(nil)
17 Y	Richard de Rupe	Tremoderet	3⅓	2 15 6	1 7 10½	1 7 8½
X	Richard de Rupa	Tremodered	3⅓	(2 15 6)	1 7 10½	[read 7½] 1 7 7½
18 Y	Henry de la Pomeray	Tregeny	1	16 8	16 8	is quit
X	Henry de la Pomerey	Treguni	1	(16 8)	16 8	(nil)
19 Y	The fief of John *de Monte Acuto* which Michael son of Nicholas holds with his wife	Elerky	1	16 8	16 8	is quit
X	The heir of John *de Munthagu*	Elerki	1	(16 8)	16 8	(nil)
20 Y	Archenbald *le Flemeng*	Bray in Devon	7	5 16 8	1 5 0	4 11 8
X	Archibald *le Flemag*	Bray	7	(5 16 8)	1 5 0	(4 11 8)
21 Y	William *de Walebrewes*	Hutbenbo	1	16 8	16 8	is quit
X	William *de Walebreu*	Hutbeno	1	(16 8)	16 8	(nil)
22 Y	Walter *de Dunstervill'*	Tybidi	1	16 8	16 8	is quit
X	Walter *de Donastanfile*	Thibidi	1	(16 8)	16 8	(nil)
23 Y	William son of Richard son of Yve	Trenowicht	½	8 4	8 4	is quit
X	William son of Richard	Trenewyd	½	(8 4)	8 4	(nil)

Reference	Tenant	Fief	Fees	Assessment £ s d	Payment £ s d	Owing £ s d
24 Y	The fief which was of Bartholomew Toret	Streton	1	16 8	16 8	is quit
X	Bert' son of Tborold	Stranton	1	(16 8)	16 8	(nil)
25 Y	William de Borard	(omitted)	2	(1 13 4)	(omitted)	(omitted)
X	(not entered)	---	---	---	---	---
26 Y	The prior of Tywardreit	(omitted)	1	(18 8)	(omitted)	(omitted)
X	(not entered)	---	---	---	---	---
27 Y	Radulf de Tony	Karneston' Bluston' & Helneston'	½	8 4	8 4	is quit
X	Radulf de Thoney	Carneton' Bluston' & Hellston	½	(8 4)	8 4	(nil)
28 Y	Walter de Godarvill'	Liscaret & Tywarneil	½	8 4	2 9 ½	5 7
X	Walter de Godarville	Leskeret & Tiwarneyl	½	(8 4)	1 10 ½	(6 5½)
29 Y	Gervase de Tintagel	Wyntynton & Tamerton	1/20	10	10	is quit
X	Gervase de Tinthagel	Merthin' Winiainton' & Thamerton	1/20	(10)	10	(nil)
30 Y	The abbot of Tavenstoke	Fees in Cornwall	4 whole fees	5 6 8	5 3 4	pays in Devon 3 4
X	The abbot of Tavistoke	Rame & Sevioc	6½	(uncertain)	5 3 4	(uncertain)
31 Y	Radulf de Solleny	Fauwyton	¼	4 2	4 2	is quit
X	Radulf de Sureni	Fawyton	¼	(4 2)	4 2	(nil)
32 Y	Henry Teutonicus	Alwartton' & Thywarnail	½	8 4	8 4	is quit
X	Henry Thieys	Alwarton' & Thywarneyl	½	(not copied further in the text)		
33 Y	The bishop of Exeter	In Cornwall	10 whole fees	13 6 8	13 6 8	is quit
X	The bishop of Exeter	(omitted)	(omitted)	(uncertain)	13 6 8	(uncertain)
34 Y	(Not entered)					
X	A memorandum that the fees of Gloucester have answered nothing to us (nobis).					

debt also given in Y. X may give the true payment received. In number 28, again, the calculation in Y of the difference between the assessment and the actual payment is self-contradictory; something is wrong there. X may be right in this matter, too; but we cannot tell.

In number 4, Herbert *de Pinu* and Walter son of William had been tenants of the *Middelond* fief, in their wives' right, under William Briwere the younger who was its tenant in chief.[21]

In number 6, there is a curious error in Y which gives a wrong assessment to the well-known seven fees Mortain of Ralph Bloyow. The assessment ought to have been £5 16s. 8d., and the debt still owing should consequently have been £1 14s. 2d.

In number 12 the five fees of Gervase originally included the manor of Bossiney which in its turn included the site of Tintagel castle. By the time this levy was made Gervase had parted with the manor of Bossiney and with the site of the castle, but the scribe of Y had not caught up with the situation and included 'Tintagel' with *Hornicote*. Earl Richard shifted the manorial centre from Bossiney to Tintagel.

In number 20 we meet the first of the two fiefs in Y whose lands lay mainly or entirely in Devonshire, though held in fee Mortain of the earldom of Cornwall.

In number 25 we meet the other Devonshire fief, held similarly by William *de Bosco Rohardi*, or *Borard*. It lay in Hempston.

In 26 we have in Y a statement that the prior of Tywardreath is tenant of a fee. The matter is somewhat obscure, but there appears, from earlier records, to have been some confusion between the tenure of the Montague family in Elerky (see number 19) and the tenure of the priory in an estate in that vicinity. Any service owed by the priory for that estate would have been due to the

---

[21] Herbert *de Pinu* and Walter, son of William, had married the sisters and co-heiresses of Thomas *de Middelton*, who had died during his minority, the last male of his name to be heir to the lordship of *Middelond*. Since 1203 the 10 fees of that fief had been held of the William Briweres, father and son, successively their tenants in chief by grant of King John (*Rotuli Chartarum*, Record Commissioners, London, 1837, p. 110). But, after the partition and attenuation of the lands and fees of the younger Briwere among his many co-heirs, Richard, Earl of Cornwall appears to have re-established, *de facto* if not *de jure*, his earldom's former suzerainty over the *Middelond* fief. Thereafter the 10 fees of *Middelond* are found being held by the *Pinu* heirs of *Middelton* of the honour of the earls and dukes of Cornwall. The intruded Briwere tenancy had been eliminated.

local landlord, not, as is implied in Y, to the earldom of Cornwall. This is perhaps the reason why the prior had paid nothing to the collectors.

I have already called attention to the omission by X of numbers 25 and 26, presumably because X is characteristically a record of receipts. But see number 32, below.

In number 28 (as in number 2) the calculations of payments received and debts still owing are incompatible. We cannot confidently amend these figures.

In number 30 the number of fees belonging in Cornwall to the abbey of Tavistock is correctly given in Y and wrongly in X. These fees, like those of the bishop of Exeter (number 33) were 'whole' fees, that is to say the large fees of Gloucester, not the small fees of Mortain. I describe the assessment and the amount owing as 'uncertain' in X (though the assessment in Y is correct) merely because its original scribe might have used wrong calculations had he worked out an assessment from his erroneous number of fees.

In 32 the appellations *Teutonicus* and *Thieys* are alternatives. This entry appears to show an exception to the concern with payments which is a characteristic of X. No payment is given there. I think, however, that the omission of the payment (which Y records) is merely accidental and that the copyist who wrote this text of X inadvertently left this entry unfinished.

In 33 (as in 30) we are dealing with fees of Gloucester. X gives no number of fees here, so no certain calculations about assessment and residual debt are implied.

Number 34, though it adds a fief to our list, is a memorandum which is not an intrinsic part of the account which X presents. The reference is to the earl of Gloucester's fief in Cornwall.

8
LIGHT ON LAMMANA

Devon and Cornwall Notes and Queries, 35 (1982-6), 281-6

IN 1983 KEITH HAMYLTON JONES discovered in a *De Banco* roll information throwing light on the obscure medieval history of Lammana. I wish to express my gratitude to Mr. Hamylton Jones for his kindness in supplying me with the text of the passage for this publication. For those readers who may not be familiar with the background against which this new information must be set I venture to give a preliminary historical outline of Lammana before presenting the new material.

Lammana was the 13th-century name[1] of a priory or monastic cell[2] in Cornwall belonging to the Somersetshire abbey of Glastonbury. The conventual headquarters—the monastic cell and its ancillary chapel—were situated on the Cornish coast next to what is now the western suburb of the town of Looe and were opposite Looe Island or, as it was then called, 'the island of St Michael of Lammana'.[3] That island, too, with the chapel of St Michael the Archangel on its summit, belonged to the Glastonbury monks. So the precincts of Lammana contained two chapels, the insular one of St Michael and the littoral conventual chapel whose dedication has been uncertain.[4] In the 13th century the name Lammana covered both.

---

[1] Whose modern form is Lemain; but antiquaries have now revived the earlier and better spelling.

[2] 'Priory' and 'cell' were sometimes interchangeable terms. Lammana was officially a priory at first.

[3] Thomas Hearne, *Adam de Domerham*, vol. II (Oxford, 1727), p. 599. This volume, cited hereafter as Hearne, contains the *Historia de Rebus Glastoniensibus* attributed to Adam de Domerham which here recites the charter of *c.* A.D. 1200 issued by Hasculf de Soleigny, a neighbouring landlord, referring to the *insulam sancti Michaelis de Lammana*.

[4] Despite its well-attested survival as a manorial chapel till 1548: even the Chantry Commissioners were confused about its location, and therefore its dedication. But the continued existence of the island chapel till that century seems to depend on the sole evidence of the coastal map of King Henry VIII's reign which depicts the chapel standing intact on the island (BL, Cotton MS, Augustus I, vol. I).

This ecclesiastical complex probably ceased to be monastic when Abbot Michael of Glastonbury alienated most of Lammana's lands (but not the conventual chapel) about the year 1250 in fee farm to the lord of the adjacent manor of Portlooe.[5] The abbey continued to appoint chaplains to Lammana until Abbot John, as will be shown below, resigned all the abbey's right in the chapel to another lord of Portlooe in 1289. With the subsequent history of Lammana this article is not concerned. It is sufficient to say that both its chapels were consigned to oblivion by the suppression of Chantries in 1548, and that both thereafter gradually disappeared.[6]

Broadly speaking, the history of Lammana after the 12th century is known: it is the earlier history which is obscure. For example, it was not known with certainty whether the place-name Lammana originally applied to a site on Looe Island, the island of St Michael of Lammana, or to the vicinity of the conventual chapel, of hitherto unknown antiquity, on the mainland. This was the more tantalising because of the historical implications of the name. It is almost certain that the first element of this Celtic name Lammana was originally the Cornish word *lan*,[7] a religious enclosure of the Celtic type sometimes called monasteries but more aptly described by Professor Charles Thomas as 'communal hermitages or perhaps eremitic communities'.[8] A Christian community of that kind might, of course, be very small, perhaps merely the huts of a few disciples beside that of their revered spiritual master, and it might have had only a transient existence. But, whatever the size or the duration of a *lan* of that sort, its essential characteristic, almost its first necessity, would have been a chapel. Though a primitive structure at first, the chapel might yet outlast the community which founded it and, being reconstructed when necessary, might survive into the Middle Ages to become a chapel of local

[5] For Abbot Michael's action see Hearne, p. 315. In 1277 an abbot of Glastonbury sued persons for breaking into the cell of Lammana (*cellam ipsius Abbatis de Lamana*) and assaulting its custodian, William de Bolevill, his monk (inform. K.H.J.; see PRO, KB27/30, *m.* 18d). This custody operated perhaps during a vacancy in the chaplaincy at Lammana.

[6] The site of the mainland chapel was excavated in 1935-6 by C.K. Croft Andrew. The site of the island chapel has never been excavated, though lately Professor Malcolm Todd viewed it and has published his comments in *Cornish Archaeology*, 22 (1983), 122-3.

[7] Compare the name of Lamorran church (*Lanmoren* 1268, *Lannmoren* 969) and also of land at the churchtown of Mevagissey parish, Lavorrick (*Lammorech*, *c.*1212). See O. J. Padel's discussion of *lann* in *Cornish Place-name Elements* (English Place-name Society, vol. LVI/LVII, 1985), pp. 142 ff.

[8] Charles Thomas, *Britain and Ireland in Early Christian Times* (London, 1971), p. 94.

devotion or a parish church. Many churches in Cornwall declare their Celtic antecedents by their own or by adjacent place-names beginning with the element *lan*.[9] Indeed, in an exceptional instance, the former name, *Lanow*, of the parish church of St Kew can be traced in documents back through *Landoho* to a 10th-century *Landochou* and finally to a Celtic 'monastery' (or *lan*) of *Docco* of the sixth century.[10] Few records of Cornwall's history before the Norman Conquest have survived: we must therefore study carefully the implications of its place-names, such as Lammana.

Not until a charter issued *c.*1200 by Hasculf de Soleigny [MS. *Solenneio*] to the monks by Glastonbury, confirming and augmenting privileges granted them by his predecessors (lords of Portlooe manor), do particulars about the monastic establishment at Lammana slowly begin to emerge.[11] The only two known earlier references to the place give no particulars and are chiefly useful in establishing the date at which Lammana was already owned by Glastonbury Abbey. The first of these two references is in the confirmation of privileges and possessions which Pope Lucius II granted to the abbey in 1144.[12] In it *Lamene* is merely mentioned as one among many other possessions of the Abbey. There is, perhaps, a probability that the context of this reference implies the existence of a chapel at *Lamene*, but that is not explicitly stated. It is, however, difficult to believe that the great Somersetshire abbey would have undertaken the maintenance of so small, remote and inconvenient a property as Lammana in Cornwall unless it was already the focus of a local cult of some distinction; and that would predicate the presence of a chapel there. The second reference is in effect a repetition of the first, found in the confirmation by Pope Alexander III in 1168 of the substance of his predecessor's *privilegium*; the spelling this time being *Lamane*.[13]

Both these documents emanated from the papal Chancery and both have survived in copies; so their spellings of this place-name are not so authoritative as the spelling *Lammana* found in a copy of the manuscript issued by its neighbour, Hasculf de Soleigny, and repeated thereafter in other records.

[9] See O. J. Padel, 'Cornish Names of Parish Churches', in *Cornish Studies*, 4-5 (1976-7), 15 ff.
[10] See chapter 1.
[11] Hearne, p. 599.
[12] *Ibid.*, p. 323.
[13] *The Great Chartulary of Glastonbury*, vol. I (ed. A. Watkin, Somerset Record Soc., vol. 59), p. 129.

Unfortunately Lammana became a bone of contention between Glastonbury Abbey and Launceston Priory. The latter monastery had acquired the parish church and rectory of Talland early in the 13th century. It found the Glastonbury monks at Lammana in possession of privileges given by lords of Portlooe manor (which was in Talland parish) and especially the valuable right to tithe the manorial demesne. These things made mainland Lammana, in effect, into an ecclesiastically separate enclave within Talland parish, to the detriment of its parish church and Launceston Priory. Successive priors of Launceston during that century persistently endeavoured to whittle away Lammana's rights and to usurp its assets and its chapel. These attempts usually resulted in judicial tribunals rejecting Launceston's pretensions. Then, in the summer of 1289, John, Abbot of Glastonbury, demised his abbey's rights in the chapel of Lammana to Walter de Treverbyn [lord of the manor of Portlooe].[14] Thenceforth until the 16th century successive lords of Portlooe remained the owners of the mainland ex-conventual chapel of Lammana. By this transaction in 1289 Walter became the impropriator of the chapel and its Great Tithes, in succession to abbots of Glastonbury who, *ex officio*, had been its impropriate rectors. Moreover, the chapel of Lammana being now vacant, Walter *ipso facto* had acquired the Abbey's right to nominate the next incumbent. But the prior of Launceston chose to lodge an objection to Walter's right to make that nomination. So Walter took the prior to court and the case was heard in November, 1289, in the Court of Common Pleas at Westminster.[15] Walter, the plaintiff, pleaded the rights of former abbots of Glastonbury at Lammana, now acquired by himself. The prior, by his attorney, had the effrontery to deny the validity of the former abbatial status at Lammana and to allege that its advowson belonged of right to Launceston Priory's church of Talland. Both assertions were false. After hearing the pleas of both parties to the action the Justices adjourned the hearing to January, 1290, in order that the sheriff of Cornwall might bring to Westminster 12 unbiassed men competent to testify what the true facts were. In the event it was not until October, 1290, that the 12 jurors appeared before the Court and the Justices were able to give judgement.[16] It was, of course, in Walter's favour. By a fortunate and unusual scribal procedure the record of that final hearing was retrospectively appended

---

[14] So stated in this lawsuit.
[15] PRO, CP40/80, *m.* 151d.
[16] *Ibid.*

(in somewhat compressed script) to the record of the first hearing on the earlier *De Banco* roll, so the substance of the whole suit can be read on a single membrane. Our present concern is only with the conclusion of this lengthy record, where the jurors' evidence and the judgement are given. I take leave to omit everything else from the following free translation of the relevant passages. The corresponding Latin text will be found below in an appendix.

> Afterwards in the quinzaine of Michaelmas in the 18th regnal year of the present King [Edward][17] the parties and the jurors came [into court] … And the jurors, chosen with the consent of both parties, say upon their oath that Lammana is a certain sea-girt island in which a certain chapel of Saint Michael used to be kept up where the abbots of Glastonbury, time out of mind,[18] had monks celebrating Divine Service. And, because in days of old many of those people who through devotion would have wanted to visit the said chapel on Saint Michael's Day often lost their lives in the stormy sea,[19] a certain chapel of Saint Michael was constructed upon the coast opposite the said island. They also say that all abbots of Glastonbury, not the said prior [of Launceston], have ever been seised of all kinds of tithes, dues and offerings chargeable against everything tithable within the aforesaid boundaries,[20] from the time the said chapel was constructed until the day on which the said John, Abbot of Glastonbury, enfeoffed the said Walter with the house and ploughland to which the said advowson pertains.[21]
>
> Therefore it was adjudged that the said Walter should recover his presentation to the said chapel and his statutory damages in respect of the lapse of two years,[22] *viz.* the value of the chapel during two years which is assessed by the jurors at 100 shillings *per annum* etc. And the same Walter may have a writ to the

---

[17] Law-days of the week beginning 15 October, 1290.

[18] Legal 'time out of mind' was time before 3 September, 1189.

[19] Looe Island has no harbour, only a small exposed beach.

[20] These boundaries, previously described in this and earlier records, extended from the estuary at Looe up the road now called West Looe Hill as far as a spring in front of Portlooe manor-house and thence by its stream down to the sea. Between these bounds and the sea-water the land rendered tithes to the impropriator and his chaplain of Lammana. Looe Island was extra-parochial and so was not referred to in these bounds which were within Talland parish.

[21] Carrucate or Ploughland means here a unit of areal measurement, not simply arable land. The size of the unit varied widely from place to place. In this instance it may refer to the field beside the mainland chapel next the ex-conventual cell. It was customary to annex an advowson to a piece of land.

[22] Perhaps the legal interpretation of the year and a half since Walter had acquired the chapel. The period had included the harvests of two years, 1289 and 1290, and the tithes of corn due to the impropriator of Lammana chapel were its most valuable perquisite.

bishop of Exeter [ordering him] to admit a suitable person to the said chapel upon Walter's presentation, the prior's counterclaim notwithstanding. And the prior is in mercy etc.[23]

There is no reason to doubt the accuracy of the jurors' evidence. They would know that tithes had been paid as recently as the previous year to the abbot of Glastonbury or his chaplain. Some jurors may have talked to Glastonbury monks or custodians at Lammana and so may have heard their monastic traditions. In any case it is certain that an event so locally important and portentous as the construction of the mainland conventual chapel of Lammana would be remembered in Talland parish and its borough of Porthpighan (later West Looe) for a longer period than had in fact elapsed since that event—at an outside estimate 150 years, but perhaps much less. So we may be confident that the original *lan* of Lammana was (as always seemed probable) situated on Looe Island and that the chapel on the mainland was a secondary and a medieval development.

Perhaps the motives of the monks of Lammana engaged in that development may not have been as altruistic as the jurors supposed. A station upon the mainland must have seemed to the monks to be much preferable to a station upon an island which, even in these days of engined boats, can be isolated by bad winter weather for two weeks at a time.

Finally we learn with satisfaction (despite the obfuscations of the Chantries Certificates) that the dedication of the mainland chapel of Lammana, like that of the island chapel, was in honour of St Michael the Archangel.

Appendix (MS. in PRO: CP40/80, m. 151 dorso)

Postea a die *san*cti Michae*li*s in XV dies anno regni d*omi*ni R*egis* nu*n*c XVIII° ven*erunt* p*ar*ces[24] et simili*ter* Jur*atores* ... Et Jur*atores* de consensu p*ar*cium[25] el*ec*ti d*icu*nt sup*er* sacr*amentu*m suu*m* qu*o*d Lammana est qued*am* insula mari clausa in qua de *san*cto Michael*e* construebat*ur* quidam [*sic*] Capella in qua Abba*tes* Glaston.[26] temp*or*e quo non excat [*sic*][27] memoria hab*ueru*nt monachos diuina celebr*ant*es & q*ui*a antiquit*us* multi eor*um* qui die s*an*cti Michae*li*s ad p*re*di*ct*am capellam causa deuoc*ionis* accedere voluissent p*er* maris intemp*er*iem sepius p*er*ieru*n*t constructa fuit quedam Capella s*an*cti Michae*li*s sup*er* litus maris ex

---

[23] At the mercy of the king for making a false claim. The penalty would be a monetary fine.
[24] *Partes.*
[25] *Partium.*
[26] Extension uncertain here and below.
[27] Recte *extat* (for *existat*).

opposito p*redicte* Insule Et d*icunt* q*uo*d a temp*ore* constructio*n*is eiusde*m* Capelle usq*ue* ad diem quo p*redictus* Joha*nn*es Abbas Glaston. p*redictu*m Walte*rum* de p*redictis* mes*uagio* & carucata te*rre* ad que p*redicta* aduoca[c]io p*er*tinet feoffa[uit] om*n*es Abba*tes* Glaston. semp*er* fu*eru*nt seysiti de o*mn*imodis decimis obuencionib*us* & oblac*ionibus* p*er*cipiendis de om*n*ib*us* reb*us* detimandis [*sic*][28] infra p*redictas* diuisas & non p*redictus* Prior Et i*deo* cons*ideratum* est q*uod* p*redictus* Walte*rus* recup*er*et presentac*ionem* suam ad p*redict*am capellam etc. & dampna sua p*er* statut*um* eo q*uo*d temp*us* semestre elabit*ur* scil*icet* valorem Capelle p*er* bienn*um* que extendit*ur per* Jur*atores* ad Centu*m* solidos p*er* annu*m* etc. Et idem Walte*rus* h*ab*eat br*e*ue ad Ep*iscopu*m Exon.[29] q*uod* non obstante reclamac*ione* p*redicti* Prioris ad p*resentacionem* p*redicti* Walte*ri* ad p*redict*am Capellam idoneam p*er*sonam admittat Et Prior in m*isericordi*a etc.

[The excavations carried out in the 1930s have now been thoroughly published: L. Olson and C. O'Mahoney, 'Lammana, West Looe: C. K. Croft Andrew's excavations of the chapel and Monks House, 1935–6', *Cornish Archaeology*, 33 (1994), 96-129, and further references. The site generally is discussed by Lynette Olson, *Early Monasteries in Cornwall* (Woodbridge, 1989), pp. 97-104. Hasculf's charter of 1199 × 1220 is printed and discussed by O. J. Padel, 'Glastonbury's Cornish connections', in *The Archaeology and History of Glastonbury Abbey. Essays in Honour of the Ninetieth Birthday of C. A. Ralegh Radford*, edited by Lesley Abrams and James P. Carley (Woodbridge, 1991), pp. 245-56 (at pp. 253-6). One important description (not necessarily accurate) of the mainland site seems to have been overlooked; it occurs in a survey of the manor of Portlooe in about 1600, printed by C. E. Welch, 'A survey of some Duchy manors', in *Devon and Cornwall Notes and Queries*, 29 (1962-4) and 30 (1965-7), as follows (vol. 29, pp. 163-4):

> The lands supposed to be demeasnes doe paie all tithes unto a demolished Chapell called le Mayne, sometimes standing upon the demeisnes lands, hard upon the Sea, whose ruinate walls in part appear with other ruines of some other buildings, which I thinck was the Scite of the Mannor house; ... This Chappell called le Mayne was erected as it seemeth as a chappell of ease for the Owners and Inhabitants of the demeisnes of the Mannor, the parish church being Tallands, distant 1½ myle from the chappel, and there was allowed a Clearke for performance of Divine service, Burying nor christning nor other divine Rites being there performed ...

O.J.P.]

---

[28] For *decimandis*—a careless transcription from the original record of this later session.
[29] Extension uncertain.

9
The Names of the Hundreds of Cornwall

Devon and Cornwall Notes and Queries, 30 (1965-7), 36-40

The earliest lists of the Hundreds of Cornwall are to be found in the Exeter Domesday Book, a volume which contains besides returns made in the course of the actual Domesday Book survey, 1086, the text of another record known as the Geld Inquest usually assigned to the year 1084, just before Domesday Book, and like it a fiscal document concerned with taxation. In the texts of the Exeter and Exchequer Domesday surveys no mention is made of any Cornish Hundreds, but in the Geld Inquest they are named. There are also two short lists of these Hundreds prefixed to the Geld Inquest, though their contents are not drawn from it, and these appear to have been added as memoranda for official use, perhaps when the present manuscript called the Exeter Domesday Book was compiled. Their date is likely to be *c.*1086.

All these records were the work of royal administrators, working through established administrative channels so far as those served them. Even the Domesday Book commissioners would inevitably have been in touch with the regular centres of fiscal administration in each Hundred, though they were independent of them.

The Saxons had administered Cornwall from various large estates, latterly manors, and these would naturally figure prominently in official documents. For this reason the Cornish Hundreds of the earliest lists all bear the names of their paramount manors, to each of which the bailiwick of its Hundred was attached. But it does not follow that these were the names by which the Hundreds were popularly known: there is indeed evidence to the contrary.

In the Geld Inquest and the two short lists prefixed to it eight Hundreds of Cornwall are given with the following names (I omit the conventional Latin case-endings of the MS.): *Conarditon* (Connerton manor in Gwithian parish), *Winnenton* (Winnianton in Gunwalloe), *Tibesten* (Tybesta in Creed), *Rielton* (Rialton in St Columb Minor), *Pauton* (Pawton in St Breoke), *Straton* (Stratton in the parish of that name), *Fawiton* (Fawton in St Neot), and *Rileston* (Rillaton in Linkinhorne): the last is also once given the alternative name *Ist* (East, for East Wivelshire), while the Hundred of *Rielton* is only briefly alluded to in the Geld Inquest (because it did not pay tax) as the land of *St Petroch*.

The century following Domesday Book saw changes in the organisation of these Hundreds and still greater changes in the nomenclature adopted in official records. The Saxon Hundred of *Straton* became divided into three separate Hundreds called (in modern spelling) Stratton, Lesnewth and Triggshire: and the two contiguous Hundreds of *Rielton* and *Pauton* were amalgamated into a single Hundred of Pydarshire. New names appeared also for all the other Hundreds. *Conarditon* became the Hundred of Penwith, *Winnenton* became Kerrier, *Tibesten* became Powdershire, *Fawiton* became West Wivelshire, and *Rileston* became East Wivelshire. In the 12th century and afterwards many of these Hundreds were usually given the termination *-scir*, *-sir*, or *-shire*, as above: Penwith, Kerrier, Lesnewth and Stratton were exceptions to this practice. At the end of these notes I will give the more important early spellings of all these names.

This change from manorial names to what became the standard ones can hardly be explained except by the assumption that an official, limited practice was discontinued in favour of a popular and traditional usage. There is evidence that this was so and that some at least of the new names had been in use in past centuries either as names of tracts of country dominating the Hundreds to which they afterwards gave their names or else as the names of the Hundreds themselves.

The name Trigg, for instance, was very ancient: it occurs in the form *pagus Tricurius* in the oldest *Vita Samsonis*, a Life of St Samson written perhaps as early as the early seventh century. In *c.*881 it is found again as *Triconscire*, when it included the district of Stratton.

When in the 12th century the name Pydarshire was applied to the united Hundreds of *Rielton* and *Pauton* a usage was being followed that must have originated before 839. Pydarshire is believed to be a form of the name 'Petroc's shire' and it described the widespread territories outside *Triconscire* belonging to the Celtic monastery of St Petroc. But by 839 St Petroc had lost for ever to a rival and episcopal landowner all that large part of those territories constituting the one-time Hundred of *Pauton*,[1] the monks retaining only the lands in the

[1] Except Padstow, the site of St Petroc's monastery itself.

Hundred of *Rielton*. As used in the 12th century the name Pydarshire was an anachronism, a survival of a traditional but no longer accurate usage.

The Hundreds of East and West Wivelshire also bear names that are clearly older than the 12th century when they first appear in records. I do not think that it has hitherto been noticed that these names almost certainly are derived from the Saxon *twi-feald-scir*, meaning 'twofold shire'. As anyone who has lived in that part of Cornwall will know, the name 'Wivel', or 'Wivelshire', *tout court*, does not exist there: it is always either East Wivelshire or West Wivelshire (though a modern literary reference to a supposed name 'Wivel' is occasionally found, as a mistaken deduction). This invariable prefixing of the words East or West to the word *wivelshire* explains what has happened to the initial letter 't' of *twi-feald-scir, scil.* (Eas)t-wivel-shire, (Wes)t-wivel-shire. For this reason I am unable to accept C. G. Henderson's suggestion that this district formed originally a single Hundred of 'Wivel': on the contrary, its characteristic from the outset was its twofold nature, as its name testifies. In this region of valleys and moorlands between the Fowey and Tamar rivers it is difficult to detect any natural geographical division sufficiently marked to account for the epithet 'twofold'. The duality inherent in the name may therefore have been a matter of jurisdiction, not of geography, and is likely to have been the partition of this otherwise more or less amorphous region into two Saxon Hundreds.

In these three instances of Triggshire, Pydarshire and East with West Wivelshire we thus find evidence of the pre-Conquest use of the names to describe large areas of land. Stratton is an ancient place-name about which more will be said; but its use as a Hundred-name is not evidenced before 1084. At an earlier date it was, as has been mentioned, included in *Triconscire*. Lesnewth, too, is likely to be a name older than the Norman Conquest: it contains the element *lys*, meaning a court, a ruler's residence, which is rare in Cornish place-names. But here again there is no evidence that the name was applied to a Hundred until that Hundred was carved out in the 12th century. Formerly it had been part of the ancient district of Triggshire and as late as 1211 Lesnewth Hundred was referred to as *Middle Trigersir*. The remaining three Hundreds of Penwith, Powdershire and Kerrier have names that all seem to be in origin names of districts, not of single places. On the analogy of the rest they are likely to have been in use at least as early as the Saxon era in Cornwall, but there is no information about them before the Norman

The Names of the Hundreds of Cornwall 79

Conquest and the names themselves are not helpful in determining their age. Penwith is a Cornish word which R. Morton Nance says means just 'end': it is the name of the extreme westerly Hundred of the County. The name Powdershire (*Poureder* in 1130) derives, I suggest, from the Cornish words *pou*, a district, and *ereder*, ploughs, having reference to a region distinguished at an early date by its comparatively advanced state of cultivation. That could have been an apt description of this exceptionally fertile Hundred. The name Kerrier has defied all attempts at interpretation.

The introduction of Hundreds was the work of the Saxons, whatever names were given; but in Cornwall, as in the rest of England, the date at which the introduction was made is obscure. Henderson has pointed out that in Cornwall the Hundreds were created at once and did not grow up casually from Celtic tribal divisions, and that there is evidence of this in the fact that the four western Hundreds all meet together at one point and 'are obviously intended to divide western Cornwall into four quarters as far as geographical features will allow'.

Here, in italics, is a list of the most important early spellings of the names borne by the Cornish Hundreds. In brackets are added further examples of the same names applied to places or districts as distinct from Hundreds. The suffix '-ton', when it appears, represents the Saxon 'tun', meaning 'homestead', 'village'.

PENWITH HUNDRED: *Conarditon*, 1084; *Conarton*, 1086; (Kenarton, 1238; Connertone, 1259; Connerton, 1284).
Penweth, 1201; *Penwith*, c.1200. Meaning 'end'.
KERRIER HUNDRED: *Winneton*, 1084, 1086; (Winneton, 1086; Winielton, 1177; Winienton, 1187, 1202; Wynielton, c.1235; Wynyenton, 1236; Wynyanton, 1333. Now Winnianton.)
Kerior, 1201; *Kariel*, 1215; *Kerier*, 1284. Meaning unknown.
POWDERSHIRE HUNDRED: *Tibesten*, 1084; *Tibestern*, 1086; (Tibesteu [for Tibesten], 1086; Tibesten, 1185; Tybbestein, 1227; Tibeste, 1284; Tybeste, 1337. Later Tybesta.)
Poureder, 1130; *Pourdescira*, 1188; *Porede*, 1201; *Powrdesir*, 1201; *Poudreshyre*, 1284. Perhaps from Cornish *pou-ereder*, signifying a district of arable land.
PYDARSHIRE HUNDRED: *Pidelescira*, 1188; *Pidelesir*, 1201; *Pydreshyre*, 1284. The name is believed to come from Pedyr, possibly a form of Petroc.

Pydarshire Hundred comprised the two earlier Hundreds of:
Rielton, 1086; called the lands of St Petroch, 1084; (Rielton, c.1270; Rialton, 1333.

The name seems to signify a ruler's residence, or capital estate, from Cornish *real*, royal, supreme.)

Pauton, 1084, 1086; (Polltun, 909, *c*.984 referring to an MS. of *c*.838; Polton, 1243; Pouton, 1311; Powtone, 1383; now Pawton, meaning the homestead by a pool.)

TRIGGSHIRE HUNDRED: *Trigerscire*, 1130; *Trigelesir*, *Trigesir*, 1201; Trigesyre, 1222; *Tryggershyre*, 1284; (the district was called the *pagus Tricurius*, *c*.625, and *Triconscire*, *c*.881.)

LESNEWTH HUNDRED: *Lisniwet*, *Lisneweth*, 1201; *Middle Trigersir*, 1211; *Lysnewythe*, 1284. From Cornish *lys-noweth*, 'new court'.

STRATTON HUNDRED: *Straton*, 1084, 1086; *Stratton*, 1201. The name is not derived, as is often asserted, from Saxon *stræt*, meaning 'street' or roman road; nor does it come from a river there called the Strat—a late name which Henderson denounced as 'a popular attempt to define the name Stratton'. That stream's original name is found in 13th-century documents as *Neat*, *Neth*, or *Nehet*, a Celtic name cognate with the river-names Nidd in Yorkshire and Nedd or Neath in Glamorgan. Stratton was called *Strætneat c*.881, showing that the first element, despite its spelling, must be the old Cornish word *strat*, a stream [strictly 'valley', O.J.P.], not the Saxon *stræt*. Later Saxons added their customary suffix making the name *Stret-neat-tun*, now Stratton.

WEST WIVELSHIRE HUNDRED: *Fawiton*, 1084, 1086; (Fauiton, 1149; Fauton, 1198; Fawyton, 1241; the name derives from the river *Fawi*, or Fowey.)

Westwiueleswapentagio, 1188: *Westwiuelesir*, 1201; *Westwiuelesire*, 1284. For the meaning see above.

EAST WIVELSHIRE HUNDRED: *Rileston*, 1084; *Rillecton*, 1130; (Ridlaton, 1076; Risleston 1086; Rillatun, *c*.1170; Relaton, 1197; Ridlacton, 1221; Rillaton, 1337. The first element is Cornish *rid*, later *ris*, a ford; the second element may be Cornish *lys*, a court, but the forms giving it as *lat* do not support this.)

Ist, 1086; *Estwiuelesir*, 1201; *Estwevelesir*, 1215; *Estwyueleschir*, 1284; For the meaning see above.

[When this essay was written an article by Charles Thomas, 'Settlement-history in early Cornwall, I. The antiquity of the Hundreds', *Cornish Archaeology*, 3 (1964), 70–9, had not yet appeared. The two complement each other. Subsequent writers have endorsed the derivations given above, particularly that for Eastwivelshire and Westwivelshire; and Thomas's derivation of Trigg as an ancient tribal name, 'three-tribe people', *Tricorii* (compare Gaulish *Petrucorii*, 'four-tribe people') has also found general acceptance. The citations of Henderson on pp. 78-9 refer to 'A note on the hundreds of Powder and Pyder', in Charles Henderson, *Essays in Cornish History* (Oxford, 1935), pp. 108-24 (on p. 108). O.J.P.]

10
THE EARLIEST BOROUGH CHARTER OF EAST LOOE

Journal of the Royal Institution of Cornwall, n. s., 8 (1978-81), 350-7.

Introduction

In the year 1320 Sir Oto of Bodrugan, knight, lord of the manor of Pendrim in St Martin by Looe parish, inspected, ratified and promulgated over his own seal the charter of liberties which his great-great-great grandmother, Lucy *Rossel* or Russell, lady of Pendrim, had granted to her free men of the little Cornish town of Looe (now East Looe) and Shutta about a hundred years earlier. By it she created this seigneurial or manorial borough; and Oto's charter, reissuing hers, became its principal governing instrument until it was superseded in 1587 by a Crown charter of incorporation bestowing greater independence and wider liberties upon the inhabitants.

The manuscript of Lucy's original charter was probably neglected after Oto's had been procured, and has long since vanished. Oto's charter itself was lost to general view for a very long period, perhaps as much as 250 years, consequent upon its own supersession in 1587; but it reappeared in 1936, somewhat damaged, among documents from Trelawne in Pelynt parish, the former home of the Trelawny family.[1]

It is evident that at some period this parchment has been stored in damp conditions, perhaps at the bottom of a wooden chest, whereby damp stains and dirt have considerably disfigured the left margin and a few words. Moreover it has suffered violence, for a rectangular piece has been torn, apparently deliberately, from a top corner, taking with it the concluding words of five lines of writing. We may be confident that this treatment was not inflicted at Trelawne, where the Trelawnys took care of their great collection of ancient manuscripts and, until these were finally dispersed, maintained them in good condition. The probability is that a member of the Trelawny family, which

[1] It is deposited in the Royal Institution of Cornwall at Truro.

provided Recorders to the borough of East Looe during the fifty years or so before 1734, rescued the charter from imminent peril at Looe and removed it to Trelawne for safe keeping. Be that as it may, we can be sure that Oto's charter owes its preservation to that fortunate migration.

Technically the document is a chirograph (though it will be convenient to continue referring to it as a 'charter'), being one of a pair of indentures such as would constitute an agreement between two or more parties. In this instance the parties were Oto, of the one part, and the burgesses of East Looe, of the other part, who had been at odds over what Oto considered to have been their encroachment upon his land and their misappropriation of rent due to him from Shutta. By these indentures the burgesses, on their part, desiring to procure this charter and to resolve the conflict, undertook not to claim under earlier charters than this, if any such should be discovered, granted to the borough by Oto's ancestors. Oto, on his part, acceding to their entreaties, reissued the charter granted by his ancestress, Lucy Russel, to the burgesses of the said town which he referred to as a 'free borough'.

This document from Trelawne is the grant which Oto sealed (it has a single label or tag for a seal, from which the wax has now gone) and which the burgesses of East Looe kept: its counterpart, sealed, as the text informs us, with no less than 14 seals, would have been retained by Oto, but is not known to be extant.

The text of Lucy Russel's charter, contained in that of Oto which is printed here, is therefore a copy, though it seems to be a careful one (judging, for instance, by the spelling of proper names in it). Apart from the damage already described, this manuscript shows some wear in its creases; but the writing, though somewhat faded, is clear except for the missing letters and words. Fortunately almost all the torn-off words can be supplied with certainty, either from their repetitions in the text or by means of a word for word English translation of this Latin text. This translation seems to have been made by a certain Richard Trethenack in 1531; it was the only version of the charter known to Thomas Bond, the careful and knowledgeable Town Clerk of East Looe. Curiously enough Trethenack's translation which Bond printed in 1823[2] was in one or two particulars inferior to a copy of it which remained in the

---

[2] Thomas Bond, *Topographical and Historical Sketches of the Boroughs of East and West Looe* (London, 1823), pp. 260 ff.

Town Hall until this century. His translation proves to have been faithful by standards of his own day, except for place-names which he often misread quite shockingly.

Lucy Russel's charter cannot at present be dated precisely, for instance from personal names it mentions (though nearly all of them, except those in the boundaries section, appear and reappear in other records of the earliest decades in the 13th century).[3] Nevertheless a *terminus a quo* is provided by John of Trenoda among the witnesses. This man, the first of several so named, cannot have obtained his manor of Trenoda, which descended to his heirs, before the death, in or shortly before October 1212, of its previous tenant, Drogo of Vernun [*alias* of Trenoda] whose relict, Alice, then received dower therein.[4] Thereafter she and the said John each quit-claimed land in the manor contemporaneously.[5] Less secure as a *terminus ad quem* (though supported to some extent by what is known and shown below about Henry of Bodrugan) is an inference from the presence as a witness of Richard [of] *Cersyaus* [*alias* Cereseals, *alias* Ceriseaus, and later Sergeaux]. Richard was already a knight in the year 1201,[6] was living in 1214,[7] but may have been dead by September 1229, when Andrew of Cereseals, his successor, was active in the county.[8]

Henry of Bodrugan, Lucy's son and heir, was a defendant in a plea of Novel Disseisin in 1221,[9] was suing for lands in April, 1225,[10] and for some of his inheritance (at Treworrick in St Ewe parish) in 1229[11] (though it is not certain that he had by then inherited his mother's manor of Pendrim). With others he had been employed by the king on 30 January, 1223, to sell timber from royal estates in Cornwall.[12] According to Sir John Maclean he was sheriff of Cornwall in the 10th and 11th years of the reign of King Henry III

---

[3] I don't recollect meeting Turstan of Hendresuk again alive: he was dead and his son was lord of Hendresuk in 1250. Nor am I sure that I have encountered Wymund of Hay, unless under a misspelt christian name. These two men were witnesses.
[4] *Rotuli Litterarum Clausarum*, I (ed. T. D. Hardy, 1833) p. 124b.
[5] *Launceston Cartulary*, [edited by Hull, nos. 486-7].
[6] Selden Soc., vol. 68, no. 454.
[7] *Curia Regis Rolls*, vol. VII, 94.
[8] *Cal. of Patent Rolls*, Henry III, vol. II (see 1229, 30 August–6 September).
[9] *Ibid.*, Henry III, vol. I (see 1221, 16 August).
[10] *Rot. Litt. Claus.* II (T. D. Hardy, 1844), p. 26a, 6 April.
[11] *Cal. of Patent Rolls*, Henry III, vol. II (see 1229, 10 September).
[12] *Ibid.*, Henry III, vol. I (see the date cited).

[Michaelmas to Michaelmas 1225-6 and 1226-7].[13] So Henry of Bodrugan must by then have been an adult of repute and position in the county. He was still living in 1256, his latest certain date. On 24 March, 1237, Henry had obtained the king's licence to have a weekly market on Fridays and an annual fair on the eve, feast and morrow of Michaelmas in his manor of *Pendrun*:[14] these were established in his borough of East Looe. All things considered, if we assume that Lucy Russel's charter was issued by her about the year 1220, we shall probably not be more than a few years wrong either way.

The Latin text of Oto of Bodrugan's charter of 1320, printed here, contains customary contractions and suspensions: I have extended them in italics. Also in italics, but enclosed within square brackets, are letters and words supplied by me where they are illegible or missing in the manuscript. The scribe chose to use one or other of two characters each representing either of our small letters 'u' and 'v' when these are initially placed (excepting only the word *vel*): but as that choice was erratically and inconsistently exercised I have had to ignore its vagaries and have printed 'u' or 'v' as the sense required. On the other hand, when the letters 'u' and 'v' occupy mediate positions, and also in the word *vel*, he consistently wrote a third character for both: I have printed it as 'u'.

Text

OMNIBUS CH*RIST* I fidelibus ad quos p*r*esens scriptum p*er*uenerit Oto de Bodrugan miles d*ominus* de Pendrem et Loo salutem in d*omi*no Nouerit Uniuersitas vestra q*uo*d cum quedam contenciones mot[*e*[15] *essent inter Henricum de Lym Johannem Hadmer Johannem Dyala Adam*] Jerman Nichola[*u*]m de Lomond Thomam Fountayn Roger*u*m de Lomond Reginaldu*m* Chepman[16] Joha*nn*em Symon Thomam Forst Walter*u*m de Lym Joha*nn*em Vigros et Ric*ardu*m de Bodkenuer tunc p*re*positum ville Et [[17]*omnes alios burgenses de Loo ex una parte Et nos predictum Otonem*] ex p*ar*te altera sup*er* quibusdam p*ro*presturis sup*er nos* p*er* p*re*d*ict*os Burgenses factis p*er* diu*er*sa loca In manerio nostro de Pendrem

---

[13] Sir John Maclean, *History of ... Trigg Minor*, I, 548 and note.
[14] *Cal. of Charter Rolls*, I (see date cited).
[15] Torn off.
[16] The initial letter of this oft repeated surname generally resembles 'T' more than 'C', but he appears as Reginald *Chapman* at East Looe in 1327.
[17] Torn off.

Et etiam de redditu Viginti solidoru*m* p*er* p*re*di*ct*os Hen*ric*u*m* de Lym Joh*ann*em Hadmer J[*ohannem*[18] *Dyala Adam Jerman Nicholaum de Lomond Thomam Fountayn*] Roger*um* de Lomond Reginaldum Chepman Joh*ann*em Symon Thomam Forst Walter*u*m de Lym Joh*ann*em Vigros et Ri*cardu*m de Bodkenuer Et omnes alios Burgenses p*re*di*ct*os appropriato Et Versus nos [[19] *ad dehereditationem nostram in villa de La Suta conselato Predicti autem*] Hen*ric*u*s* de Lym Joh*ann*es Hadmer Joh*ann*es Dyala Ad*am* Jerman Nich*ol*au*s* de Lomond Thomas Fountayn Roger*us* de Lomond Re*g*inaldu*s* Chepman Joh*ann*es Symon Thomas Forst Walter*us* de Lym Joh*ann*es Vigros et Ri*card*u*s* de Bo[*dk*enver[20] *et omnes Burgenses*] p*re*di*ct*ar*um* villarum nobis attencius [[21] *suppli*]carunt q*uo*d de p*re*di*ct*is transgressionibus cu*m* eis misericordit*er* dispensaremus et fa[*ct*]um Lucie Rossel et Ph*i*l*i*pp*i*[22] de Bodrugan antecessor*um* nostror*um* eis confirmare Curaremus. Nos tandem p*ro* Salute anime nostre et omniu*m* antecessor*um* nostror*um* di*ctorum* Burgensiu*m* peticioni fauentes Inspeximus cartam di*ctorum* Lucie et Ph*i*l*i*pp*i* In hec verba.

> Sciant p*re*sentes et fut*u*ri q*uo*d Ego Lucia Rossel d*omi*na de Pendrem consensu et assensu Henr*ici* de Bodrugan filii mei unigeniti dedi concessi om*n*ibus liberis hominibus nostris de Loo et de La Suta totam t*er*ram nostram in villa de Loo et de La Suta p*er* has metas videlic*et* a quadam petra que vocat*ur* Serpatorre iuxta Kekkeshaye versus orientem sup*er* falasiam Et sic p*er* fossatos ortor*um* de Loo antiquitus factos usq*ue* ad angulu*m* orti Walt*er*i de Lym iuxta ortu*m* Joh*ann*is de Martistowe conuenc*i*onarii n*os*t*r*i de Pendrem una cu*m* quodam orto qui vocat*ur* prallynghissay qui continet in se extra metas p*re*dic*t*as vinginti[23] p*er*ticatas t*er*re Et sic ab orto p*re*di*ct*i Walt*er*i per vet*er*es fossatos usq*ue* ad Regalem viam que tendit de Loo versus maneriu*m* nostrum de Pendrem Et sic p*er* Regalem viam descendendo usq*ue* ad fossatum parci nostri qui vocat*ur* Lelordispark versus Borialem cu*m* tota t*er*ra infra eundem parcu*m* Et sic de Cornera p*re*di*ct*i parci

---

[18] Torn off.

[19] Torn off but reconstructed from Trethenack's translation, assisted by his failure to recognise that *conselato*, or perhaps *consulato*, in his exemplar meant *concelato*, 'concealed'. His consequent translation of it by the incomprehensible word 'consulate' puzzled Thomas Bond, but is nevertheless informative.

[20] Torn off the 5th line.

[21] Partly torn off the 5th line, but the descenders of the letters 's' and 'pp' remain, as also the feet of the two minims of the intervening letter 'u', thus indicating the Latin word which Trethenack translated 'besoughte'. The written remnant of the verb, *-carunt*, is a contraction of *-caverunt*, 'have entreated'.

[22] A strange scribal error, for in the following charter his name is Henry, not Philip (who was Henry's son).

[23] *Sic*, for *viginti*.

per Rupes linialiter descendendo usque ad angulum gardini Thome Le taillur In villa de La Suta Et sic a dicto angulo ascendendo versus orientem includens totum parcum Thome Le taillur Et a cornera boriali pred[icti p]arci linialiter descend[end]o usque ad gardinum Henrici de Lym Et sic per fossatum dicti gardini Includens totum parcum Johannis Dyala usque ad magnum Iter de La Suta Et abinde includens omnes ortos de La Suta versus partem occidentalem usque ad mare Habendam et tenendam totam predictam terram predicfis hominibus et heredibus suis de nobis et heredibus nostris libere quiete et hereditarie inperpetuum. Et ad illam cum pertinentiis sine calumpnia uel contradictione nostri uel heredum nostrorum Dandam uel vendendam quandocumque uel Cuicumque voluerint Reddendo inde nobis et heredibus nostris per annum Centum solidos argenti ad festum Pasche. Concessimus etiam et volumus quod prefati homines nostri de Loo et da La Suta nobis uel Balliuis nostris Creditum faciant ad valenciam decem solidorum de omni mercandysa que in eadem villa inuenitur ad terminum [qua]draginta dierum et si ultra eundem terminum predictum debitum per nos uel Bailliuos [nostr]os detentum fuerit prefati homines non teneantur nobis uel Balliuis nostris amplius Creditum facere nisi ipsi voluntarie voluerint donec omne debitum eis persoluatur Concessimus etiam predicfis hominibus quod releuium pleni mesuagii videlicet quarte partis unius acre anglicane terre non excedat triginta denarios. Concessimus etiam quod prefati homines et eorum heredes quieti sint et inmunes de omni tallagio et auxilio sicut burgenses aliorum Burgorum de Cornubia. Et quod habeant redditum omnium censariorum dictarum villarum in auxilium redditus supradicfi. Ita quod nos uel heredes nostri non teneamur eos tensare. Et quod [prep]ositus villarum predictarum per comunem electionem annuatim eligatur Et post annum com[p]letum amoueatur Ita quod quicumque pro tempore fuerit prepositus nobis et heredibus nostris de redditibus et omnibus aliis exitibus predictarum villarum in fine anni fideliter respondeat et Compotum reddat. Volumus etiam et concedimus quod Curia predictarum villarum a quindena in quindenam teneatur et per diem Lune per Balliuum nostrum et non per alium. Et quod placita predicfe Curie per decretum et consilium omnium Burgensium predictarum villarum deducantur et terminentur Et quod nullus forinsecus possit habere tabernam in prefatis [vil]lis nisi fuerit in comuna et libertate earumdem villarum. Ita tamen quod emende assise panis et ceruisie fracte nobis et heredibus nostris plene fiant secundum quod antece[sso]ribus nostris fieri consueuit cum omnibus aliis seruiciis debitis et consuetis. In cuius rei testimonium presenti scripto sigilla nostra apposu[i]mus. Hiis testibus Ricardo Cersyaus Ricardo de Kylgadh Augero de Tregeryek Willelmo filio Baldewyni Turstano de Hendresuk Roberto Crothard[24] Roberto de Ludcotte Johanne de Trenoda Wymundo de Hay et multis aliis.

---

[24] His name was really Crochard, but the scribe read the letters 'ch' in his exemplar as 'th'.

Nos autem prefatus Oto volumus pro nobis et heredibus nostris quod predicti Henricus de Lym Johannes Hadmer Johannes Dyala Adam Jerman Nicholaus de Lomond Thomas Fountayn Rogerus de Lomond Reginaldus Chepman Johannes Symon Thomas Forst Walterus de Lym Johannes Vigros et Ricardus de Bodkenuer et alii Burgenses in dictis villis comorantes predictas donaciones et libertates ac liberas consuetudines ipsis hominibus et eorum heredibus eis succedentibus de nobis et heredibus nostris habeant et teneant inperpetuum. Et illas eis pro nobis et heredibus nostris concedimus et confirmamus omni tempore futuro duraturas Et volumus quod predicti Henricus de Lym Johannes Hadmer Johannes Dyala Adam Jerman Nicholaus de Lomond Thomas Fountayn Rogerus de Lomond Reginaldus Chepman Johannes Symon Thomas Forst Walterus de Lym Johannes Vigros et Ricardus de Bodkenuer et omnes conburgenses predictarum villarum et eorum heredes liberii burgenses nostri sint et liberum Burgagium habeant in villis predictis cum omnibus que ad libertatem liberii Burgii pertinent quantum in nobis est sicut predicta carta superior testatur Et Nos predicti Henricus de Lym Johannes Hadmer Johannes Dyala Adam Jerman Nicholaus de Lomond Thomas Fountayn Rogerus de [Lomon]d Reginaldus Chepman Johannes Symon Thomas [For]st Walterus de Lym Johannes Vigros et Ricardus de Bodkenuer pro nobis et aliis [c]onburgensibus nostris de predictis villis de Loo et de La Suta pro ista confirmatione et pro istis transgressionibus pacificandis volumus pro nobis et heredibus nostris quod omnes alie Carte et [s]cripta nobis uel antecessoribus nostris facte ante datam presentis scripti per aliq[u]em antecessorum predicti Otonis domini nostri si que inposterum inueniatur quod omnino irritentur [eua]cuentur et pro nullis habeantur. Ut autem hec nostra concessio et presentis scripti confirmacio Robur inperpetuum optineat firmitatis eidem scripto admodum Cyrografhy confecto tam sigillum predicti Otonis domini nostri quam sigilla Henrici de Lym Johannis Hadmer Johannis Dyala Ade Jerman Nicholai de Lomond Thome Fountayn Rogeri de Lomond Reginaldi Chepman Johannis Symon Thome Forst Walteri de Lym Johannis Vigros et Ricardi de Bodkenuer Una cum comuni sigillo Burgensium dictarum villarum alternatim sunt appensa. Hiis testibus dominis Willelmo de Botriaus Henrico de Campo Arnulphi Johanne de Carmynou militibus Johanne de Trenoda Augero de Fursdone Osberto Hamely Ricardo de London' Herberto de Skewyek Johanne clerico Et multis aliis Data apud Loo die veneris In festo beati Petri quod dicitur aduincula Anno Regni Edwardi filii Regis Edwardi quartodecimo.

Translation

To all the faithful of Christ to whom the present writing shall have come Oto of Bodrugan, knight, lord of Pendrem and Loo, gives greeting in the Lord. Be it known to you all that whereas there have been certain differences arising between Henry of Lym, John Hadmer, John Dyala, Adam Jerman, Nicholas of Lomond, Thomas Fountayn, Roger of Lomond, Reginald Chepman, John Symon, Thomas Forst, Walter of Lym, John Vigros, and Richard of Bodkenver[25] then the portreeve of the town, and all the other burgesses of Loo, of the one part, and Us, the aforesaid Oto, of the other part, touching certain encroachments made upon Us at divers places in Our manor of Pendrem and also touching twenty shillings rent appropriated and concealed from us in the town of The Suta to our disherison by the aforesaid Henry of Lym [etc.] and all the other aforesaid burgesses; Now the aforesaid Henry of Lym [etc.] and all the burgesses of the aforesaid towns have the more diligently entreated Us mercifully to pardon them and their aforesaid offences and to be ready to confirm the deed of Our ancestors, Lucy Rossel and Philip[26] of Bodrugan; Therefore We, approving the petition of the said burgesses, for the welfare of Our soul and of those of all Our ancestors, Have inspected the charter of the said Lucy and Philip in these words:

> Know all men present and to come that I, Lucy Rossel, lady of Pendrem, with the consent and assent of Henry of Bodrugan, mine only son, have granted to all our free men of Loo[27] and of The Suta[28] all our land in the town of Loo and of The Suta having these boundaries: Namely from a certain stone[29] called

---

[25] Bokenver farm in the same parish as East Looe, rather than the obscure Buckenver cottage in Morval. The name, containing the frequently ambiguous letter-combinations 'nn' or 'nu', appears here to be written Bodke*nn*er (instead of Bodke*nu*er). But we may be confident that such was not the writer's intention, because no known Cornish place-name was being spelt Bodkenner then, if indeed any ever rightly was.

[26] See note 22.

[27] Now East Looe.

[28] Shutta, a hamlet formerly separate but now a part of East Looe.

[29] Or 'rock', or even 'crag'.

Serpatorre[30] next Kekkeshaye[31] on the east upon the cliff; And so by the ancient hedges[32] of the gardens of Loo as far as the angle of the garden of Walter of Lym next the garden of John of Martistowe,[33] our conventionary tenant of Pendrem, with a certain garden called Prallynghissay[34] which contains within it outside the aforesaid boundaries twenty perches of land; And so from the garden of the aforesaid Walter by the old hedges as far as the King's highway[35] from Loo to our manor of Pendrem; And so down the King's highway as far as the hedge of our field called Lelordispark[36] on the north together with all the land inside that field; And so from the corner of the aforesaid field downwards along the rocks as far as the angle of the orchard of Thomas the tailor in the town of The Suta; And so from the said angle going up eastwards including all the field of Thomas the tailor; And from the north corner of the aforesaid field straight down as far as the orchard of Henry of Lym; And so by the hedge of the aforesaid orchard including all the field of John Dyala as far as the main road of The Suta;[37] And thence westward to the sea[38] including all the gardens of The Suta. To have and to hold all the aforesaid land to the aforesaid men and their heirs of us and our heirs freely, quietly and hereditarily forever. To

---

[30] *Serpatorre*, this important place has not been identified: probably it had disappeared into the sea before 1531 when Trethenack translated this bound-mark as 'Paine rocke next kekysheire'. Pen or Paine Rock, a tidal rock at the seaward eastern edge of Looe beach, has been the first-named bound of East Looe borough ever since. But when Lucy Russel's charter was written there was almost certainly a low peninsula (still faintly indicated) running out as far as Pen Rock, so that *Serpatorre* may have stood above the rock. Similar land formations ([30] *contd.*) formerly existed in bays on both sides of Looe, where coastal erosion has been and still is astonishingly rapid. Even during the present writer's lifetime he has seen meadowland or tilled plots on the seaward side of public roads disappear into the sea at Millendreath and Talland beaches, followed by the roads themselves!

[31] *Kekkeshaye* 'upon the cliff'—either the cliff of the lost peninsula or that of the coastal hill rearwards at Looe beach. But erosion has continuously been changing the face of that coastal hill, even since Bond wrote in 1823, so that it is useless to seek the site of this 'hay' or enclosure.

[32] *Fossatos* is here and below translated as 'hedges', as the terrain seems to preclude the alternative meaning of 'ditches'.

[33] *Martistowe* or Martinstow was evidently the name of the precincts of the church of St Martin by Looe near Pendrim manor-house.

[34] An unidentified 'hay' or enclosure.

[35] The ancient road from Looe to Barbican, Pendrim and Liskeard.

[36] 'The Lord's field'.

[37] Now Shutta, where the open water-shoot alongside the road, which probably produced the place-name, existed until 1963.

[38] *Usque ad mare*, to the seawater in the estuary. Except for a later extension of these boundaries, after reaching Shutta, to include the Common Wood, the boundaries here described were probably those of the borough of East Looe throughout its existence. When East Looe was severed from the ecclesiastical parish of St Martin by Looe in 1845 the extended boundary of the borough became the new parish boundary, which can be followed on maps until 1979 when this ecclesiastical boundary was abolished.

have it with its appurtenances, free from claim or gainsaying by us or our heirs, to be given or sold whensoever and to whomsoever they may wish. Rendering thence to us and our heirs yearly one hundred silver shillings at Easter. We have granted also and it is our will that our aforesaid men of Loo and of The Suta may allow credit to us or our bailiffs, for a period of forty days, up to the value of ten shillings for all merchandise which is available in the same town: And if the aforesaid debt be carried forward by us or our bailiffs beyond that period, the aforesaid men may not be obliged to extend further credit to us or our bailiffs, unless they voluntarily wish to, until all the debt be paid to them. We have granted also to the aforesaid men that the relief[39] for a complete homestead, that is to say a quarter of an English acre of land, may not exceed thirty pence. We have granted also that the aforesaid men and their heirs may be quit and immune from all Tallage and Aid,[40] like the burgesses of other boroughs of Cornwall. And that they may receive the rent of all shopkeepers of the said towns in aid of the aforesaid rent, So that neither we nor our heirs may be obliged to levy the charge on them. And that the portreeve of the aforesaid towns may be elected each year by common choice, and that he may be removed after a full year. So that whoever shall have been portreeve for the time being may answer faithfully and may render account to us and our heirs for the rents and all other issues of the aforesaid towns. It is also our will and we have granted that the Court of the aforesaid towns may be held fortnightly on a Monday by our bailiff and by none other, and that the pleas of the aforesaid Court may be introduced and concluded by the decree and advice of all the burgesses of the aforesaid towns. And that no stranger may have a shop in the aforesaid towns unless he shall have been within the commune and liberty of the aforesaid towns. Provided however that the correction of breach of the Assize of bread and ale may belong wholly to us and our heirs, as it was wont to belong to our ancestors, with all other services, debts and customs. In witness whereof we have affixed our seal to the present writing. With these witnesses, Richard Cersyaus,[41] Richard of Kylgadh,[42] Aucher of Tregeryek,[43] William son of Baldewyn, Turstan of Hendresuk,[44] Robert Crothard,[45] Robert of Ludcotte,[46] John of Trenoda,[47] Wymund of Hay[48] and many others.

[39] A sum payable upon succession to a free tenement or burgage.
[40] Tallages and Aids were financial levies.
[41] Lord of Lanreath manor.
[42] Lord of Killigarth manor.
[43] Tregarrick in Pelynt.
[44] Hendersick in Talland.
[45] Of Treworgy in Duloe. See note 24.
[46] Lydcott in Morval.
[47] Trenode in Morval.
[48] Hay, a lost hamlet at Hay lane, near Looe.

The Earliest Borough Charter of East Looe

Now We, the aforesaid Oto, on behalf of Ourself and Our heirs, are willing that the aforesaid Henry of Lym [etc.] and other burgesses residing in the said towns may continue to have and hold the aforesaid grants, liberties and free customs for themselves and for their successive heirs from Us and Our heirs forever. And We, for Us and for Our heirs, have granted and confirm to these men and their heirs that those things shall endure for all time to come. And it is Our will, so far as in Us lies, that, as the aforesaid charter testifies, Henry of Lym [etc.] and all fellow-burgesses of the aforesaid towns and their heirs may be Our free burgesses and may have free burgage in the aforesaid towns with all things pertaining to a free borough.

And for this confirmation and in order that these offences may be allayed it is the will of us, the aforesaid Henry of Lym [etc.] for us and for our other fellow-burgesses of the aforesaid towns of Loo and of The Suta, that all other charters and writings made to us or our ancestors before the date of the present writing by any ancestor of the aforesaid Oto, our lord, if any such be found hereafter, may be invalidated, annulled and set at naught for us and our heirs. Moreover, in order that this our grant and ratifying confirmation of the present writing may be for ever affirmed, the seal of the aforesaid Oto, our lord, as well as the seals of Henry of Lym [etc.], together with the common seal of the burgesses of the said towns, have been affixed alternately to the same writing, purposely made as a complete chirograph. With these witnesses, Sir William of Botriaus, Sir Henry of Champernoun, Sir John of Carmynou, knights, John of Trenoda, Aucher of Fursdone, Osbert Hamely, Richard of London, Herbert of Skewyek, John the clerk and many others. Given at Loo[49] on Friday, the feast of St Peter's Chains, in the fourteenth regnal year of Edward, son of king Edward [1 August, 1320].

---

[49] The words 'Given at *Loo*' were possibly formal and not factual. The names of the witnesses, several of whom were not landowners near Looe, suggest that this document was sealed at some assembly elsewhere, perhaps at Bodmin or Launceston.

11
THE DESCENT OF THE DEVONSHIRE FAMILY OF WILLINGTON FROM ROBERT, EARL OF GLOUCESTER

MANY RECORDS of the Willingtons of Gloucestershire and Devonshire survive from the 150 years before the senior male line failed in 1396; this study, however, will attempt to trace from scantier records of earlier ages some of the family's remoter and obscurer ancestors during the century following the death in 1147 of Robert, earl of Gloucester, one of its progenitors on the distaff side. For the convenience of readers place-names cited in the following pages will usually be given in their modern spellings. Some of the records referred to in the notes will be quoted, partially or wholly, in the Appendix. In these pages references will be made to three estates or fiefs whose tenures provide genealogical evidence: they may conveniently be introduced at this point.

The least regarded of them—they were of widely differing consequence—was the manor and liberty of Connerton in Cornwall. Its titular capital was in the parish of Gwithian, but its liberties encompassed the hundred of Penwith at the Land's End.[1] In Domesday Book Connerton manor was royal demesne assigned to the use of Queen Matilda;[2] but by the beginning of the 12th century it had been infeudated to a tenant in chief and by the year 1155 it had been further subinfeudated twice. Its tenants held it by knight's service of their immediate overlord who, before the end of the 12th century, was the tenant of the Devonshire manor and honour of Umberleigh.

The manor and honour of Umberleigh, the second of the three estates referred to above, had its capital in the Devonshire parish of Atherington in the hundred of North Tawton where the Willingtons, like some of their forebears who will appear in these pages, had their principal residence. During

---

[1] P. A. S. Pool, 'The Penheleg Manuscript', *Journal of the Royal Institution of Cornwall*, n. s., 3 (1957-60), 163-228 (especially pp. 165-7).
[2] *Domesday Book seu Liber Censualis* (London, 1783), I, fol. 120, *Conarditone*; *Domesday Book* (general editor John Morris), 10, *Cornwall*, edited by C. and F. Thorn (Chichester, 1979), 1.14.

the latter decades of the 12th century a number of estates and knight's fees in Cornwall, including among them the service of one knight from the tenant of Connerton, became annexed to Devonshire or other fees pertaining to Umberleigh so that Umberleigh became, in effect, a sub-honour of the great honour of Gloucester of which it was held by the service of 16 knight's fees.

The third estate or fief referred to was the honour of Gloucester itself. This huge estate, the appendage of the medieval earldom of Gloucester, extended into many English counties besides Gloucestershire, Devonshire and Cornwall.[3] It seems to have originated in a grant of lands made by King William the Second to his loyal baron, Robert FitzHamon.[4] This augmentation of FitzHamon's original barony descended to his daughter Maud, whom King Henry I made FitzHamon's heiress and married to his own favourite but illegitimate son, Robert, whom his father created earl of Gloucester in 1122 and who afterwards became famous as the skilful general and mainstay of Robert's half-sister, the empress Maud, in her war with King Stephen. It was perhaps about the time of Earl Robert's marriage with Maud that the term 'honour of Gloucester' became current.

Robert, earl of Gloucester, had several children and was succeeded on his death in 1147 by his eldest son, William. Among Earl Robert's younger sons was one, also named Robert, who has been unnoticed by some historians, though (as will appear) he is mentioned in documents. His brother, Earl William, once referred to him as 'Robert of Ilchester', but usually he is called Robert, son of Earl Robert of Gloucester, or Robert, brother of Earl William. He must not be confused with his nephew, Robert, son of Earl William, a youth who died in his father's lifetime.

The earliest mention of this Robert, son of Earl Robert of Gloucester, appears to be in a charter whose substance is preserved in a cartulary of Tewkesbury Abbey.[5] The document records an enactment by Earl William of Gloucester reciting that his father, Earl Robert, before his death had given all his eight churches and chapels in Cornwall to his clerk, Picard, who, immediately after Earl Robert's death, had besought Earl William to transfer

---

[3] *The Red Book of the Exchequer*, edited by Hubert Hall, 3 vols (London, 1896), II, 607-10; also I, 288-92.

[4] *The Ecclesiastical History of Orderic Vitalis*, edited by Marjorie Chibnall, 6 vols (Oxford, 1969-80), IV, 220; [also I. J. Sanders, *English Baronies* (Oxford, 1960), p. 6. O.J.P.]

[5] British Library, MS. Cotton Cleop. A.vii, fol. 76; see Appendix, no. 1.

them to the priory of St James of Bristol. The document further records that Earl William, complying with Picard's request, declared that he made this transfer before he gave 'the land of Cornwall' to his brother, Robert of Ilchester. The phrase 'the land of Cornwall' is not further defined in this instrument, but its context requires that it should include all those estates in Cornwall whose occupation in his own demesne enabled Earl William to give their (identifiable) churches and chapels to the priory of St James with a good title; which he could not have done after he had given away those demesne lands to Robert of Ilchester. It may be mentioned here that the misinterpretation of this document which supposes Robert of Ilchester to have been the brother not of Earl William but of Picard is contrary to its grammar.[6]

This copy in the Tewkesbury cartulary of Earl William's charter (despite its imperfections noticed in the Appendix, no. 1) is important to students of Cornish history for its ecclesiastical and its unique feudal information. With its grantor's letter of intendance which follows (see Appendix, no. 2), it is the only direct evidence that Earl Robert of Gloucester had held in demesne eight estates in Cornwall, situated where their churches and chapels stood, and that his son and successor, Earl William, gave some or all of those eight estates to his own brother, Robert, who consequently became for a time a major, though hitherto unrecognised, landlord in the feudal hierarchy of mid-12th-century Cornwall.[7] Proof of the existence of this Robert, son of Earl Robert of Gloucester, by no means depends solely on the evidence of the foregoing document; he is named as brother of Earl William in three extant charters, in one of which, moreover, the dowager countess of Gloucester, Mabel, described William and Robert as her sons.[8] There also is (or was in 1805 when it was printed) the text of a charter issued by the man himself, Robert, son of Earl Robert of Gloucester. By it in about the year 1155 he granted his demesne manor of Connerton to a certain Richard *Pincerna*, 'the butler', to hold to him and his heirs by the service to Robert and his heirs of

---

[6] *Earldom of Gloucester Charters*, edited by R. B. Patterson (Oxford, 1973), p. 170 (no. 202).
[7] Little is yet known of the processes by which Cornish estates of the honour of Gloucester became annexed to the Devonshire sub-honours of Winkleigh and Umberleigh.
[8] Patterson, *Earldom of Gloucester Charters*, nos. 48, 96 and 171.

The Descent of Willington from Robert, Earl of Gloucester

Family Tree
showing the descent of Umberleigh
(Holders of Umberleigh are underlined)

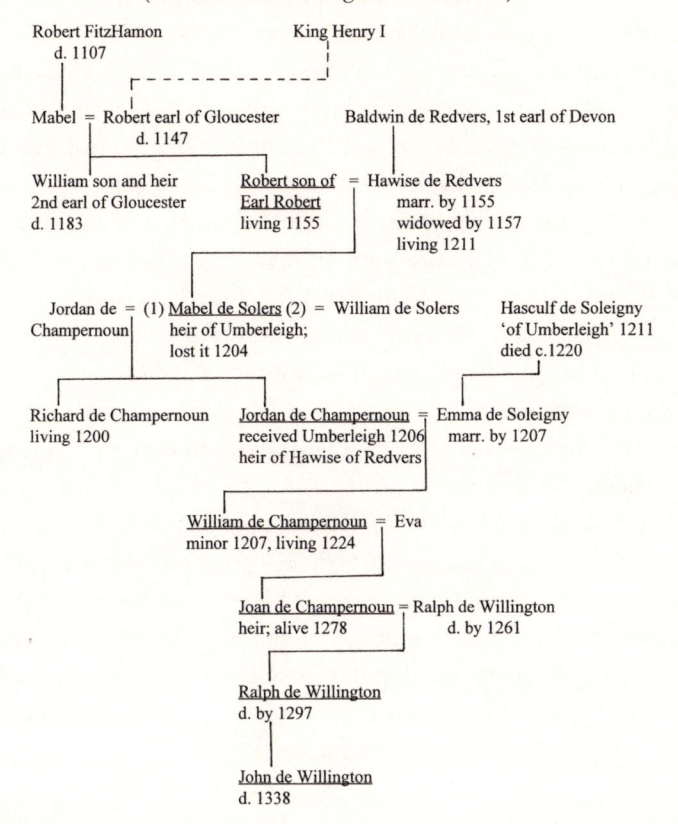

```
Robert FitzHamon                King Henry I
    d. 1107                          |
       |         _____|
       |        |
Mabel = Robert earl of Gloucester        Baldwin de Redvers, 1st earl of Devon
              d. 1147                             |
       _____|_____                        |
      |                   |                       |
William son and heir    Robert son of  =  Hawise de Redvers
2nd earl of Gloucester  Earl Robert       marr. by 1155
    d. 1183             living 1155       widowed by 1157
                                          living 1211

Jordan de = (1) Mabel de Solers (2) = William de Solers   Hasculf de Soleigny
Champernoun     heir of Umberleigh;                       'of Umberleigh' 1211
                lost it 1204                              died c.1220

Richard de Champernoun    Jordan de Champernoun = Emma de Soleigny
living 1200               received Umberleigh 1206  marr. by 1207
                          heir of Hawise of Redvers

                    William de Champernoun = Eva
                    minor 1207, living 1224

                        Joan de Champernoun = Ralph de Willington
                        heir; alive 1278      d. by 1261

                            Ralph de Willington
                            d. by 1297

                            John de Willington
                            d. 1338
```

one knight's fee.[9] This grant may be said to foreshadow the descent of the Willingtons from its grantor, Robert, because in later centuries they are found to be the recipients of that feudal service due from tenants of Connerton to Robert's heirs. In effect the Willingtons came to stand in the shoes of those heirs: this study endeavours to discover why they wore them.

Robert's grant of Connerton to Pincerna was confirmed by his kinsman, King Henry II,[10] and the king's confirmation was many times inspected by

---

[9] Charles Bowles, *A Short Account of the Hundred of Penwith in the County of Cornwall* (Shaftesbury, 1805), pp. 19-20; see Appendix, no. 3.

[10] Bowles, *Hundred of Penwith*, pp. 21-2; see Appendix, no. 4.

monarchs or their ministers because the liberties of the manor of Connerton infringed the Crown's prerogatives. For instance, at the Cornish eyre of 1284, when the then tenant of Connerton, the heiress Alice de Lanherne, claimed its liberties, the king's Justices called for the production of the original charter granting the manor of Connerton to Richard Pincerna as well as for King Henry's confirmation, inspecting them before ratifying her claims. These documents were again inspected and ratified at the Cornish eyre of 1302; and Queen Elizabeth in 1579 inspected and by her letters patent confirmed to John Arundell, tenant of Connerton, the charters of confirmation of King Henry II and others.[11]

Robert, son of Earl Robert, was probably dead before the Carta of his brother, Earl William, was compiled in 1166, for there is no mention of him in that list of the earl's military tenants. Instead, the tenant then of the fee of Umberleigh, subsequently possessed by Robert's daughter and heiress and her descendants, was a certain Jordan de Champernoun who was probably sometime her husband.[12] Robert, son of Earl Robert of Gloucester, had married Hawise de Redvers (*Redveriis* and *Ripariis*), daughter of Baldwin de Redvers, first earl of Devonshire. Throughout her long life—she was still living in 1211[13]—this lady used the style Hawisia de Redvers in preference to her husband's name, even when witnessing his own charter granting Connerton to Pincerna. Evidently she was proud of her lineage; indeed before she died she could boast of being the daughter of one, the sister of two, and the aunt of two more earls of Devonshire.[14] The texts of several of her charters have survived, many of them relating to her manor of Fleet in Dorset.[15]

---

[11] 1284 Eyre Roll, Public Record Office, Just.1/111, m. 25 (see Appendix, no. 7); 1302 Eyre Roll, PRO Just.1/117, m. 67d; 1579 Confirmation Roll, PRO C.56/98, m. 12.

[12] *Red Book of the Exchequer*, I, 291. [See below, n. 19.]

[13] *Devon Feet of Fines*, edited by O. J. Reichel, F. B. Prideaux and H. Tatley-Soper, 2 vols, Devon and Cornwall Record Society (Exeter, 1912-39), I, 38 (no. 62).

[14] Baldwin died in 1155; his son Richard died in 1162; Richard's son Baldwin died in 1188; his other son Richard died in *c.*1191; their uncle William de Redvers alias William de Vernon (brother of Earl Richard I) died in 1217.

[15] The Cartulary of Christchurch Priory, Twynham, Hampshire (British Library, MS. Cotton Tib. D. vi, vol. II) contains charters issued by her; see also notes 27-9, below. Since the foregoing was written Dr. Robert Bearman has edited the corpus of Redvers charters, including those of Hawise, in *Charters of the Redvers Family and the Earldom of Devon, 1090-1217*, Devon and Cornwall Record Society, n. s. 37 (1994) (see nos. 111-20). In no. 111 she grants land in Puddletown (Dorset) to Quarr Abbey, along with her husband Robert, 'son of the earl of Gloucester'. [Compare also p. 187, note to no. 15. O.J.P.]

Robert, son of Earl Robert, with his wife Hawise de Redvers had a daughter named Mabel, heiress of both her parents. Mabel was presumably husbandless when, by her Christian name alone, she issued a charter to John FitzRichard confirming to him her father's grant of Connerton to his father, Richard Pincerna;[16] but it is as Mabel de 'Solers' (*Soliers, Solariis*), that she usually appears in English records, notably in the Pipe Rolls.[17] In 1197 she was named as the mother of William de Solers,[18] one of an Anglo-Norman family possessing estates on both sides of the Channel until the loss of Normandy.

But this Solers marriage was not Mabel's first; she had previously been married to one of the Champernouns who (though not explicitly declared so in any record known to this writer) was probably that Jordan de Champernoun who held the fee of Umberleigh in 1166 and who must be identified with the man of that name who was witnessing charters round about the middle of the 12th century, in particular charters associated with the Devonshire family of Tracy and with Barnstaple in that county.[19] By her Champernoun marriage Mabel de Solers had two sons, Jordan de Champernoun and Richard de Champernoun (*Campo Ernulfi, Campo Arnulphi, Cambernof*). About the period 1189 × 1199 Richard de Cambernof issued a charter, concerning property in Normandy, which was subsequently confirmed by a charter of Jordan de Cambernof, his brother.[20] Richard also acted as attorney for his mother, Mabel de Solariis, in 1200 when she was engaged in a lawsuit about land in Loggans (MS. *Lug*),[21] a place in the Cornish parish of Phillack close to Connerton. (The church of Phillack, by the name *Egglosheil*, had been one of those given

---

[16] Bowles, *Hundred of Penwith*, pp. 22-4; see Appendix, no. 5.

[17] e.g. in the Pipe Roll for 1192, 4 Richard I (Pipe Roll Society, n. s. 2), p. 298; and subsequently in other years.

[18] *Feet of Fines of the Seventh and Eighth Years of the Reign of Richard I*, PRS 20 (1896), p. 55 (no.76). By 1200 this William de Solers appears to have been succeeded by Richard de Solers (Pipe Roll of 1200, 2 John, PRS n. s. 12, p. 200), whose three coheirs had inherited by 1207 (Pipe Roll of 1207, 9 John, PRS n. s. 22, p. 60; also that of 1211, 13 John, PRS n. s. 28, pp. 6 and 185).

[19] G. Oliver, *Monasticon Dioecesis Exoniensis* (Exeter, 1846) pp. 199-200, no. 5 (dated 1146); *Catalogue of Ancient Deeds*, vol. VI (London, 1915), no. C.4092; and *Historia et Cartularium Gloucestriae*, edited by W. H. Hunt (London, 1865), no. 727. [Dr. Robert Bearman has drawn attention to a charter copied into the Montebourg cartulary (Paris, Bibliothèque nationale, MS. Lat. 10087), p. 202, in which Mabel names Jordan de Campo Arnulfi and William de Soliers as her husbands, thus proving the surmise made here. O.J.P.]

[20] J. H. Round, *Calendar of Documents Preserved in France* (London, 1899), p. 195, nos. 562-3.

[21] *Curia Regis Rolls*, I, 264.

by Mabel's grandfather, Earl Robert, to his clerk, Picard.) In 1201 Mabel de Solers paid in the honour of Gloucester part of her debt on 16 knight's fees (which characterised the honour of Umberleigh) for King John's second scutage.[22]

In the same year she fined with the king in 69 marks for 16 knight's fees in lieu of service abroad.[23] Committed as she then was to the Solers family in Normandy, she was inevitably classified as a 'Norman' in 1204,[24] and so forfeited all her inheritance in England, including the manor and honour of Umberleigh. She may indeed already have made her final exit from England before she excused herself as being overseas in 1201 at the Cornish assize.[25] At the same assize she failed to appear to prosecute Hugh de Beauchamp for land in Binnerton in the Cornish parish of Crowan.[26] (The manor of Binnerton was held of her honour of Umberleigh and its chapel was another of those given to Picard). It may have been after Mabel's forfeiture of her English lands that her mother, Hawise de Redvers, ceased naming Mabel as her heiress, as she had done earlier,[27] substituting instead Mabel's son, Jordan de Champernoun,[28] her own grandson (though in the event he predeceased Hawise).[29] Before leaving Mabel de Solers the reader's attention is called to a document containing a statement irreconcilable not merely with the genealogy presented in these pages but also with all relevant records known to this writer. It appears to contain a copyist's error of a common type and will be discussed in the Appendix, no. 6, under the heading 'Confirmation by Mabira, lady of Maisoncelles.'

---

[22] Pipe Roll of 1201, 3 John (PRS n. s. 14), p. 47.

[23] *Rotuli de Oblatis et Finibus … tempore Regis Johannis*, edited by T. D. Hardy (London, 1835), p. 152.

[24] *Book of Fees*, 3 vols (London, 1923), II, 1268 (retrospective of 1252, concerning Hanford, in Dorset).

[25] *Pleas before the King or his Justices 1198-1202*, II, *Rolls or Fragments of Rolls from the Years 1198, 1201 and 1202*, edited by D.M. Stenton, Selden Society, 68 (London, 1952), p. 41 (no. 186).

[26] *Pleas before the King*, edited by Stenton, p. 153 (no. 548).

[27] Sir William Pole (Devonshire antiquary, died 1635), MS. 'Book of Evidences' (Antony House, Cornwall, MS PG/B2/6), p. 537; charter printed by Bearman, *Charters of the Redvers Family*, p. 146 (no. 114).

[28] MS. formerly in the writer's collection, now in the Royal Institution of Cornwall, Truro; printed by Bearman, *Charters of the Redvers Family*, pp. 146-7 (no. 115).

[29] Christchurch Cartulary (see above, n. 15), vol. II, fol. 8v.; printed by Bearman, *Charters of the Redvers Family*, pp. 148-9 (no. 118).

After Mabel de Solers's forfeiture of it, the manor of Umberleigh was at first set to farm by the farmer of the honour of Gloucester, William de Faleisia;[30] but in 1206 King John restored the estate to her son, Jordan de Champernoun.[31] This restitution, by a king not conspicuous for benevolence towards contumacious Norman families, needs an explanation: we may reasonably assume that the restitution was due to current political exigencies. King John was at war with Philip of France, and in that war one of John's valuable assistants was a man named Hasculf de Soleigny (*Soleigneio*).[32] This person, formerly lord of Dol and of Combourg in Brittany and territorially connected with Courseulles and elsewhere on the Channel coast of Normandy, had fled to England, we are told, 'because of the wrath of the French king':[33] he left behind him in Brittany his eldest son, John de Dol, but brought with him his other children, Ralph de Soleigny, Geoffrey de Soleigny, Iseult, and Emma. Hasculf had inherited from his father, John de Soleigny (who, like Hasculf, had served English kings), two valuable Cornish manors (of which more below), though he made his home at Kilmersdon in Somerset.[34] For a short time at the beginning of King John's reign Hasculf de Soleigny had been classified as a 'Norman', but he was rapidly accepted as a partisan of King John and was indeed entrusted, as its Warden, with the defence of the island of Jersey—a key post in the war with France and one which he held from 1207 till 1212.[35] Such a man would be in a position to press the claims of his family, in particular those of his daughter Emma who had married Jordan de Champernoun. The king's writ to the sheriff of Devonshire, ordering the restitution to Jordan de Champernoun of his mother's land of Umberleigh, specifically stated that the land should include the house as a residence for Jordan's wife.[36] In that provision for Emma's welfare we may surely see the influence of her father, Hasculf de Soleigny.

[30] *Rotuli de Oblatis et Finibus*, p. 333.
[31] *Rotuli Litterarum Clausarum*, edited by T. D. Hardy, 2 vols. (London, 1833-44), I, 68.
[32] Subligny in the Avranchin.
[33] Dom. G. A. Lobineau, *Histoire de Bretagne* (Paris, 1707), II, col. 151 (confirmation by John de Dol, son of Hasculf de Soleigny, of a grant by the latter).
[34] *Rotuli Litterarum Clausarum*, I, 17, forfeiture of Kilmersdon (*Kinemersdon*, misprinted as *Finemersdon*).
[35] Pipe Roll of 1209, 11 John (PRS, n. s. 24), p. 145 ('in passagio Hasculfi de Sulenni'); and *Rotuli Litterarum Patentium*, edited by T. D. Hardy (London, 1835), I, 90b (1212; Philip d'Aubigny replaced Hasculf as Warden of Jersey).
[36] See note 31 above.

This marriage of Emma de Soleigny with Jordan de Champernoun was the originating cause why, more than sixty years afterwards, their granddaughter, Joan de Champernoun, wife of Ralph de Willington, inherited from Geoffrey de Soleigny, Emma's last surviving brother, large portions of the two Cornish manors of Fawton and Lanteglos by Fowey. They were held by knight's service, as a feudal unity, of the honour of Launceston castle in fee Mortain: but in the 14th century jurors at certain Devonshire inquisitions post mortem, finding these two manors in the possession of the Willingtons of Umberleigh, mistakenly concluded that they were held of the honour of Umberleigh in fee Gloucester, like Connerton and the rest of the Cornish fees of Umberleigh.[37]

The date of the death of Jordan de Champernoun, son and heir of Mabel de Solers, is not precisely known but was perhaps in 1211 or 1212, as is suggested by two documents. In one of them, an account of the honour of Gloucester editorially dated 1211-12, he is named as tenant of the 16 knight's fees (of Umberleigh);[38] while in the other document the investigators of lands of 'Normans' placed Hasculf de Soleigny at Umberleigh in 1210-12.[39] The two accounts can be reconciled very simply if we assume that, when Jordan died within those years, Hasculf obtained custody of the person and lands of Jordan's son and heir, William de Champernoun, Hasculf's own grandson, known to have been a minor when his father, Jordan, died (see below).

William de Champernoun, however, cannot have remained in his minority very long after 1212. In 1216, as grandson and heir of Mabel de Solers, he recovered such seisin as she had held in Binnerton in Cornwall.[40] Then in 1224 William was summoned by the prior of Christchurch, Twynham, to warrant a charter (it is copied in that priory's cartulary and in a royal

---

[37] e.g. *Calendar of Inquisitions Post Mortem*, VIII, no. 177 (John de Willington, in 1339); and IX, no. 428 (Hugh le Despener, lord of the honour of Gloucester, in 1349). For the feudality of Fawton and Lanteglos by Fowey manors see *Calendar of Inquisitions Miscellaneous*, II, no. 511; and *Book of Fees*, I, 437. [On the large fees of the honour of Gloucester, and the smaller fees Mortain (five-eighths the size), see O. J. Reichel, "'Fees of the bishop of Exeter" in "Testa de Nevil"', *Transactions of the Devonshire Association*, 34 (1902), 566-74 (p. 570); O. J. Reichel, 'Feudal baronage', in *Victoria History of the County of Devonshire*, I (1906), 551-72 (pp. 570 and n. 4); and for the relative sizes, *Inquisitions and Assessments relating to Feudal Aids*, 6 vols (London, 1899-1920), I, 385. O.J.P.]

[38] *Red Book of the Exchequer*, II, 607.

[39] *Red Book of the Exchequer*, II, 559.

[40] *Rotuli Litterarum Clausarum*, I, 274.

confirmation) by which Hawise de Redvers had given the priory her estate of Fleet (saving a portion earlier bestowed elsewhere). William protested that she had previously given that estate to Jordan his father (who died when William was still under age), and that the charter produced by the prior was made—if it was made—by Hawise when she was old, feeble and residing at the priory.[41] In the pleadings of that suit Hawise is described as William's *atavia*, strictly meaning great-great-great-grandmother but evidently used there in a general sense as 'ancestress'; for she was only his great-grandmother. In 1229 William de Champernoun brought a writ of darrein presentment against the abbot of Tewkesbury for the churches of Umberleigh and High Bickington in adjacent Devonshire parishes.[42]

By Eva his wife William had a daughter and heiress, Joan de Champernoun. She married Ralph de Willington, sprung from a Gloucestershire stock and perhaps the man of that name who was sheriff of Devon in 1254. From their union issued the Willingtons of Devonshire and Gloucestershire of the line that terminated at the close of the 14th century, bringing this study to its conclusion. Like her ancestress, Hawise de Redvers, Joan, daughter of William de Champernoun, used her maiden name in her widowhood and was addressed by others as Lady Joan de Champernoun.[43] According to Sir William Pole, who saw coats of arms on their seals, she and her descendants, the Willingtons, abandoned their Willington arms in favour of her Champernoun ones.[44] Joan made Umberleigh her headquarters and in its chapel endowed a chantry for the souls of herself and her relations (naming her mother, Eva).[45] She was still living in 1278 when her nominee was instituted to the church of Beaford in Devon.[46] Litigation involving her grandson, John de Willington, son of her son Ralph, has provided the particulars of their descent from Emma de Soleigny.[47]

---

[41] *Bracton's Note Book*, edited by F. W. Maitland, 3 vols. (London, 1887), III, 28-9 (no. 979). Compare Bearman, *Charters of the Redvers Familiy*, p. 149n.

[42] *Patent Rolls of the Reign of Henry III*, II, *A.D. 1225-1232*, p. 288.

[43] *Calendar of Charter Rolls*, II, 267-8, misprinted as a masculine name, though the MS. has *Domine Johanne de Chaumbernoun* (PRO, C.53/71, m. 3).

[44] Sir William Pole, *Collections towards a Description of the County of Devon* (London, 1791), p. 422.

[45] Pole, MS. 'Book of Evidences' (see n. 27, above), p. 505.

[46] *The Registers of Walter Bronescombe (A.D. 1257-1280), and Peter Quivil (A.D. 1280-1291), Bishops of Exeter*, edited by F. C. Hingeston-Randolph (Exeter, 1889), p. 113.

[47] e.g. PRO, De Banco roll, C.P.40/103, m. 62.

The same John de Willington, having been fortunate to have escaped with his life after implication in the earl of Lancaster's rebellion in 1322, died in 1338 still in possession of estates.[48]

Appendix

No. 1

Confirmation by William, Earl of Gloucester, of Picard's gift of Cornish Churches to the Priory of St James, Bristol. (See illustration, lines 4-13.) This charter has been printed before, e.g. by W. Dugdale, *Monasticon Anglicanum*, new edition, 6 vols in 8 (London, 1817-30), II, 69a (no. XXII); but the names are not all accurately reproduced. The same list of churches appears, in good spellings, in a confirmation by Edward I, made in 1300, of an earlier confirmation by Henry II, made in 1175-9: Bristol Record Office, MS. 5139(488); compare *Calendar of Charter Rolls 1257-1300*, p. 488 (references owed to the kindness of Dr. Nicholas Vincent).

Date: circa 1148.

Source: Cartulary of Tewkesbury Abbey (British Library, MS. Cotton Cleop. A.VII, fol. 76).

Carta W(illelmi) Comitis Gloucestrie testificantis quod R(obertus) Comes pater suus dederat Picardo clerico suo omnes ecclesias terre sue de Cornubia cum capellis et pertinenciis suis videlicet ecclesiam de Egglosbrec, ec(clesiam) Commart(on), ec(clesiam) de Egglosheil, ec(clesiam) de Egglossant, ec(clesiam) de Eggloscrauuen et capellam de Bennart(on), ec(clesiam) de Menelidan et capellam sancti Gennot: quas omnes idem comes statim post mortem patris sui ad preces predicti Picardi dedit ecclesie beati Iacobi Bristoll' ad uictum ibidem monachorum deo seruientium ubi corpus eiusdem comitis patris sui requiescit, dicens se fecisse hanc donacionem predictis monachis antequam dedisset terram memoratam Cornubie Roberto de Iuelsestr' fratri suo.

Comment

Egglosbrec: Breage church.

Commart(on) (for *Connarton*): Gwithian church.

Egglosheil: Phillack church.

Egglossant: Sancreed church.

Eggloscrauuen: Crowan church.

---

[48] *Calendar of Inquisitions Post Mortem*, VIII, no. 177.

British Library, Cottonian MS. Cleopatra A. vii, Cartulary of Tewkesbury Abbey, fol. 76 (detail) reproduced by kind permission of the British Library Board.

capellam de Bennart(on): a chapel formerly at Binnerton in Crowan parish.
Menelidan: Trevalga church.
capellam sancti Gennot (for *Germoc*'): Germoe church.
Iuelsestr': Ilchester.

Tewkesbury Abbey was the parent house of the Priory of St James of Bristol. It is difficult to determine the probable original text of this document, though its purport is sufficiently evident. Some of Picard's part in the transaction is recognised, yet, contradictorily, the subordinate clause of this text makes Earl William appear to be the actual donor of these churches to the priory of St James. No doubt the earl might have been so, had Picard first surrendered those churches to him in order to fortify his gift by making it a magnate's. But that is not asserted; and indeed it is more probable that no. 2 (below) is correct in describing this charter as a confirmation of Picard's gift. If so, the cartulary copyist appears to have attempted to supply that fortification which Picard omitted. It will be seen that Earl William's insistence on his possession in demesne of the land containing the Cornish churches was relevant whether he was acting as donor or as confirmer.

No. 2

Notification by Earl William of Gloucester to his barons and men of his confirmation of Picard's gift.

Date: circa 1148.

Source: Cartulary of Tewkesbury Abbey, British Library, MS. Cotton Cleop. A.VII, fol. 76v.

Carta W(illelmi) Comitis missa omnibus baronibus suis et hominibus testificantis quod R(obertus) Comes pater suus dederat in elemosinam Picardo clerico suo atque nutrito omnes ecclesias terre sue in Cornubia cum capellis et omnibus pertinenciis suis. Et eo defuncto idem Picardus pro anima domini sui et sui ipsius dedit easdem ecclesias deo et ecclesie sancte Marie de Theok' et ecclesie sancti Iacobi de Bristoll' et monachis ibidem deo seruientibus saluo suo tenemento dum uiueret; et ipse Comes hanc concessionem Picardi confirmauit.

Comment

This appears to be a straightforward, though curtailed, version of an appropriate charter of intendance, entered in the customary *oratio obliqua* format. One thing is certain: nos 1 and 2 were not jointly and fraudulently compiled by a monastic hand. Had they been so, their author would have taken special care to make them agree explicitly with one another in their accounts of Earl William's part in the transaction, instead of being contradictory. [The word *nutritus*, used to describe Picard, is of interest, suggesting that Picard had been a close protégé or even foster-son of Earl Robert. O.J.P.]

No. 3

Grant by Robert son of (Robert) earl of Gloucester to Richard Pincerna of the manor and liberty of Connerton.

Date: 1154-5.

Source: Charles Bowles, *A Short Account of the Hundred of Penwith in the County of Cornwall* (Shaftesbury, 1805), pp. 19-20.

ROB. Fil Com. Glouc. — Omnibus dnis. suis et heredibus et amicis et hominibus Francis et Angl. et Walensibus tam futuris qm. presentibus sal. sciatis me dedisse et conæssisse [*sic*] Ricardo Pincerne in feodo et hereditate sibi et heredibus suis de me et de meis heredibus tenend. totum manerium meum de Cunarton cum omnibus libertatibus et pertinentiis suis excepto Penburci et Leugan et serviciis Philippi de Chaul et serviciis Aluredi de Trevi et enoc et excepta terra duorum rusticorum qm. dedi Stepho de Bello Campo in escambio pro terra Thome Archarum mei et exceptis 11 solidatis terre quas dedi Alured Marescallo contra terra Eggolphi quare volo et firmiter percipio qd. ipse et heredes sui teneant et habeant de me et de meis heredibus libere et quiete et honorifice per servicium 1 militis in bosco et in plano in pratis et pascuis in viis et semitis in aquis et terris et mariscis in ecclesiis et nominatim boscum de Drym cum hundredo et libertatibus et pertinentiis et consuetudinibus eidem manerio pertinentibus et in omnibus rebis [*sic*] et de hac donacione debeo ei perquirere consensum Willi. Com. Gloec. et ejus carte confirmationem et etiam libertatis et consuetudinis prenominato manerio pertinentes per posse meo rationabili sibi debeo perquirere et hanc donationem sibi feci pro homagio et servicio suo et pro eadem donationem predictus Ricardus dedit m. quadragint marc. argenti et unum pannum de Sera et Hawise sponse mee 1 palfridum et preterea x marcs. argenti m. accommodante. T. Hawiso [*sic*] de Redvs. sponsa mea et Walt Capellano meo, et Will de Croil et Hug. de Log. et Will. fil. Warun. et Alured Marescal. Jord. de Maresco et Pagano de Tmei. et Waltero filio Galfridi et Herie de Hadunesford Waltero de Morisi. Hac carta fuit aposita upud [*sic*] umblega primo anno post coronatiom H. Regis Angl. infra dictis.

Comment

No better text of this charter is known. It is reprinted here because of its importance to students, who may have difficulty in obtaining copies of Bowles's scarce book. He was a solicitor concerned with the Cornish estates of Lord Henry Arundell (see Christine North, 'The Arundell Archive', *Journal of the Royal Institution of Cornwall*, [3rd series], 1 (1991-94), 47-57, at p. 48). The quality of Bowles's transcripts of these two, now missing, documents (nos. 3 and 4) suggests that the latter were inferior medieval copies replacing genuine but perhaps dilapidated charters. The only addition here to the genealogy of Willington's ancestors is the evidence that Hawise de Redvers was at that date the wife of Robert, son of the earl. The fact of that marriage is, however, implicit in other documents cited above in the essay and quoted below.

It worth mentioning two items belonging to the realm of textual criticism. One is that the Arabic numerals used by the printer of Bowles's transcript in the phrase *11 solidatis* are clearly an error for Roman numerals reading *ii solidatis*, as is shown by Mabel's confirmation (below, no. 5) where the phrase is rendered as *duabus solidatis*. The other item is that the letter 'm.' before the word *quadragint* must surely stand for *mihi* or *michi*, although its context might at first glance suggest *mille*.

[The manuscript of this charter having been lost, the text is reprinted here exactly as it appears in Bowles's book, with all its misprints (sometimes astonishingly crass), punctuation, capitalisation (or lack of it) and lack of abbreviation-marks or expansions. Dr Vincent points out that the description *infra dictis* (read *infradicti*) for King Henry II at the end confirms, as suggested above, that the text was taken not from an original charter but from a later copy where there was also a copy of King Henry's confirmation, below.

Comments on names in the above charter: *Cunarton*, Connerton in Gwithian parish; *Penburci*, presumably Penberthy in St Hilary parish; *Leugan*, Loggans in Phillack parish; *Chaul*, Kayle in Phillack parish; *Trevi*, probably Trevethoe in Lelant parish (preferring the reading *Trevitho* in the confirmation of this charter by Robert's daughter Mabel, no. 5 below); *enoc*, *Henoc* in Mabel's confirmation; *Thome Archerum mei*, Mabel's confirmation shows that this should read *Archerii*, 'of Thomas, my archer'; *Drym*, Drym in Crowan parish. None of these places (including Drym) appears later as a tenement of Connerton manor, no doubt because of their exclusion here. O.J.P.]

No. 4

Confirmation by King Henry II of the grant of Connerton manor to Richard Pincerna by Robert son of the Earl of Glouceester.

Date: 1156-8.

Source: Confirmation Roll of 21 Elizabeth (1579), PRO, C.56/98, m. 12. (confirmation dated 16 July 1579); abbreviations silently expanded. Significant variant readings are cited from Bowles, *Hundred of Penwith*, pp. 21-2 (like no. 1, a very corrupt text). There is a further copy of this confirmation (14th or 15th century?), omitting the witnesses but otherwise closely similar, endorsed on a final concord dated 1334 (Cornwall Record Office, Truro, AR20/1).

Henricus rex Angl' et dux Norm' et Aquitan' et comes Andeg' episcopo Exon' et omnibus justiciis et baronibus et vicecomitibus et ministris et fidelibus suis Francis et Anglis et Wallensibus Cornubie et Devonie salutem. Sciatis me concessisse et confirmasse Ricardo Pincerne et heredibus suis manerium de Conartona[1] quod Robertus filius comitis Gloucestr' cognatus meus[2] ei dedit pro servicio suo. Quare volo et firmiter precipio quod ipse Ricardus et heredes sui illud manerium habeant et teneant per servicium unius militis de predicto Roberto filio comitis et de heredibus suis cum omnibus libertatibus et liberis consuetudinibus et quietanciis eidem manerio pertinentibus, in bosco et in plano, in pratis et pascuis, in aquis et molendinis, in viis et semitis, in hundredis et in omnibus rebus[3] et in omnibus locis, ita bene et in pace et libere et quiete et honorifice sicut unquam Robertus filius Hemundi[4] vel Comes Robertus avunculus meus manerium illud melius liberius quietius et honorificencius tenuit, tempore Regis Henrici aui mei, et sicut carta predicti Roberti filii comitis Gloucestr' cognati mei testatur. Preterea concedo eidem Ricardo et heredibus suis omnes alias terras et tenuras suas de quocumque eas rationabiliter habeat. Testibus Philippo Baioc' episcopo et Arn' Lexon' episcopo et Thoma cancell[ari]o et Ricardo de Hum' conest[abulario] et Manu[5] Biset Dap[ifero] et War[ino] filio Geroldi Camerario et Willelmo de Atmalio[6] et Henrico de Oilli et aliis, apud Cadom'.

Significant variant readings from Bowles
(Those obviously wrong are omitted.)
1. Conarton. 2. noster. 3. *in omnibus rebus* is repeated in Confirmation Roll 1579. 4. Hamundi. 5. Mathew [*sic*]. 6. Ancalia.

Comment
Like the other charters printed by Bowles in 1805, this document is now missing from the Wardour Castle archive. The text printed above is taken from Queen Elizabeth's confirmation in the Public Record Office. Its date must be after the king's first crossing to Normandy (1156) and before the death of Warin fitz Gerald (*c*.1158). In Bowles's text, though the names of the witnesses and their offices are frequently sadly corrupted (*Baive* for *Baiocensis*; *args.* for *Arnold*; *HUIS* for *Humez*; *Mathew* for *Manasses*; *Walter* for *Warin*; and *Cadorne* for *Cadome*), yet the rest of his text agrees very closely (and without lacunae) with that of Queen Elizabeth's inspeximus. Bowles's manuscript may have been severely damaged at its foot. In one case (*Ancalia*) Bowles's reading may be superior to that of the Elizabethan confirmation. Bowles clearly was not using the copy now in the Arundell archive, since that omits the witnesses.

Robert (whose grant King Henry confirms) being a son of Robert, earl of Gloucester (himself a son of King Henry I), was first cousin to King Henry II, son of the first Henry's daughter, the Empress Maud. The text of Queen Elizabeth's confirmation was also printed by Bowles, along with the text of another confirmation, by Richard earl of Cornwall, which the queen also confirmed on the same occasion (*Hundred of Penwith*, pp. 27-8).

No. 5

Confirmation by Mabel, daughter of Robert son of the Earl of Gloucester, to John son of Richard Pincerna of her father's grant of Connerton.
Date: 12th century; after 1154.
Source: Bowles, *Hundred of Penwith*, pp. 22-4.

Mabilla filia Roberti filii Comitis Glocestriæ omnibus dominis suis et heredibus et amicis suis et hominibus Francis et Anglicis et Walensibus tam futuris quam praesentibus salutem. Sciatis me concessisse et hac mea præsenti carta confirmasse Johanni filio Richardi Pincerne et heredibus suis de me et heredibus meis tenendum jure hereditario totum manerium de Cunarton cum omnibus libertatibus et pertinenciis suis excepto Penburn et Lugan et servicio Alvredi de Trevitho et servicio Henoc et excepta terra duorom rusticorum quam Robertus pater meus dedit Stephano de Bello Campo in escambro [*sic*] pro terra Thomæ Archerii sui et exceptis duabus solidatis terrae quas pater meus dedit Alvredo Marescallo propter terram Cigolfi. Quam [*sic*] volo et firmiter præcipio quod ipse Johannes et heredes sui prefatum manerium teneant et habeant de me et de heredibus meis libere et quiete pacifice et honorifice per servicium unius militis in bosco et plano in pratis et pascuis in viis et semitis in aquis et terris et mariscis in ecclesiis et nominatim boscum de drym et in hundredis et libertatibus et pertinenciis et consuetudinibus prædicto manerio pertinentibus in omnibus rebus. Et sicut Robertus pater meus dedit ipsum manerium Richardo patri ipsius Johannis et carta sua confirmavit. Hanc ego concessionem et confirmationem feci ipsi Johanni pro homagio suo et pro hac concessione mea et confirmatione dedit mihi prædictus Johannes triginta marcas argenti et unum palefridum de duabus marcis. Quod ut ratum permaneat illud sigilli mei impressione confirmavi. Hujus testibus Alard. filii [*sic*] Willi. Ric. de Wiche. Rich. fil Waltre —— et multis aliis.

Comment

Presumably Mabel had no husband living when she issued this charter. She married with Champernoun (probably before 1166) and subsequently with Solers; but the exact periods of those marriages are not known, neither is the date of her father's death. Original lost; the printed text is from Bowles, and reproduced exactly. The readings of some names here are superior to those in the original charter as printed by Bowles; see also the comment to no. 3.

No. 6

Confirmation by Mabira, Lady of Maisoncelles (Haute-Marne), daughter of Earl Robert, of a grant by her son Jordan de Champernoun

Date: 1164 × 1205.

Source: The cartulary of the Priory of St Stephen, Plessis-Grimoult, now in Caen, Archives de Calvados, H non coté Plessis-Grimoult, Cartulary, vol. II, no. 767. There is a somewhat inaccurate transcript by L. d'Anisy, 'Cartulaire de la Basse-Normandie' (PRO, 31/8/140 B, vol. III, p. 23), taken from the cartulary, with a witness-list added from an unknown source. I am most grateful to Dr. Nicholas Vincent for making available to me his transcript of the original (which I print here by his kindness), the text being previously known to me only through d'Anisy's transcript.

> Omnibus Christi fidelibus ad quos presens Carta pervenerit, Mabira filia Roberti Comitis, mater Iordani de Campo Elnulfi et domina Mansuncellarum, salutem in Domino. Noverit universitas vestra me pro salute anime mee et pro animabus omnium antecessorum meorum concessisse et hac presenti carta mea confirmasse ecclesie sancti Stephani de Plessicio et canonicis regularibus ibidem Deo servientibus donationem illam quam Iord(anus) filius meus fecit iamdictis canonicis de ecclesia sancti Amandi de Maisuncell' in perpetuam eleminosinam cum omnibus decimis et pertinentiis suis liberam et quietam ab omni servicio et consuetudine seculari. Testibus [Rogero Cancellario, Henrico Cantore, Jordano, Roberto et Radulfo archidiacono de Gouviz, Gisleberto Canonico, Gregorio Clerico, Ranulfo de Than [*sic*], Alexandro Bouet et pluribus aliis.]

Comment

Mabira, as a form of *Mabel*, was in vogue in Normandy at this period. J. H. Round (*Calendar of Documents in France*, p. 192) translates d'Anisy's copy of this charter, collating it with its source. Round points out that the priory's cartulary also contains a copy of Jordan's grant (which this of Mabira confirms) made in the presence of Henry, bishop of Bayeux (1164-1205). Round also suggests that Mabira's father (Earl Robert, according to the text) was Earl Robert of Gloucester. That sensible hypothesis, however, is contrary to the evidences adduced in this essay (as also to all other relevant facts known to this essayist). Consequently it is necessary to assume that the surviving text of Mabira's confirmation charter contains a simple haplographic error; namely that the copyist's eye was deceived by the proximity of the two words *Roberti* in his exemplar into mistaking the first one to have been the second one. He therefore omitted the words *filii Roberti* from the phrase, which should thus have read 'Mabira filia Roberti filii Roberti comitis'. Haplography has always been a copyist's trap, particularly in this man's name, 'Robert, son of Earl Robert'. Another example of exactly the same error occurred when he was mentioned in a document written perhaps a century after Mabira's: it will be found below, no. 7.

No. 7

Alice de Lanherne claims the liberties of Connerton manor.
Date: Easter term, 1284.
Source: 'Rex' roll of the eyre at Launceston (PRO, Just.1/111, m. 25).
[With two passages editorially emphasised]

Alicia de la Hurne clamat habere assisam panis et ceruisie in manerio de Conerton' et ratione balliue sue capit duos denarios pro leuand' [?][1] assise panis et ceruisie fracte per totum hundredum istud, et Comes Cornubie tercium denarium. Et dicta Alicia habet in eodem manerio Steppos [?][2] Tumberel' Furcas Estrauram et Punifaud', nesciunt quo warento. Et Alicia venit et dicit quod ipsa tenet manerium predictum cum libertatibus predictis de dono **Roberti quondam comitis Gloucestrie**, cuius predictum manerium cum hundredo predicto fuit, qui illud dedit cum balliua predicta et libertatibus predictis cuidam Ricardo Pincerne antecessori suo per cartam suam quam profert et que predictam donacionem testatur. Profert etiam cartam H(enrici) regis secundi consanguinei domini regis nunc, que testatur quod idem H(enricus) rex concessit et confirmauit Ricardo Pincerne et heredibus suis manerium de Conerton' quod **Robertus filius comitis Glocestrie** cognatus suus ei dedit pro seruicio suo, et quod ipse et heredes sui[3] cum omnibus libertatibus consuetudinibus et quietanciis eidem manerio pertinentibus in omnibus rebus et in omnibus locis, tenendum de ipso Comite et heredibus suis, ita libere et quiete sicut umquam Robertus auunculus ipsius Regis melius et liberius illud tenuit. Et super hoc venit Willemus de Gyselham qui sequitur pro domino Rege, et dicit quod licet predictus Comes dedisset predictum manerium cum hundredo predicto ipsa nichil ostendit de alico [*sic*, for *aliquo*] dono alicuius Regis ad quem donacio hundredi et huiusmodi regie libertatis pertinet, unde petit iudicium. Postea compertum est per [*rotulos* is struck out] confirmacionem predicti H(enrici) Regis quod idem H(enricus) Rex confirmauit predictam donacionem predicti manerii cum libertatibus predictis in qua continetur hundredum predictum. Compertum est per iuratores istius hundredi et per milites ad hoc electos [qui] dicunt super sacramentum suum quod predicta Alicia et omnes antecessores sui a tempore confectionis et donacionis predicte tenuerunt predictum hundredum simul cum manerio predicto. Et Comes presens est, et dicit quod tercia pars proficui istius hundredi ad ipsum pertinet, ut superius dictum est. Ideo predicta Alicia [eat] sine die cum manerio et hundredo et libertatibus predictis, saluo iure domini Regis cum inde loqui uoluerit.

[1] An obscure reading: perhaps *emend'* was written but altered to *leuand'*.
[2] This word is *cippos* 'the stocks' in the corresponding text in the 1302 eyre roll (Just.1/117, m. 67d.).
[3] A verb seems to be omitted here (*tenerent* or *haberent* or the like), and perhaps an object too (*illud*).

Comment

This passage in the eyre roll, though interesting to students of Cornish history, adds nothing new to the genealogy of Willington. It is, however, included here because it contains a particularly striking repetition of the scribal error which (as this essay contends) has corrupted the charter of Mabira, lady of Maisoncelles (see no. 6, above). When the scribe compiled this roll from official notes of the proceedings, he twice had occasion to refer to the grant (see no. 3, above) made by the man who was Robert, a son of Robert the former earl of Gloucester, but which he first says was the grant of *Roberti quondam comitis Gloucestrie*, thus confusing the son with the father. Fortunately his second reference corrects this haplographic misreading of his source; he then correctly describes the man as *Robertus filius comitis Glocestrie* (incidentally betraying unawareness of his previous lapse, as he does not correct it).

Acknowledgements

I am very grateful to those who, in one way or another, have assisted the preparation of this essay. In particular I wish to thank the authorities of the British Library for permission to print the enlarged photograph of the charter shown in the Appendix, no. 1; and those of the Public Record Office, now at Kew, for permission to print the record appearing in the Appendix, no. 7. Dr. Robert Bearman has saved me from entering two erroneous dates in footnote 14; and Mr. Keith Hamylton Jones first drew my attention to the De Banco roll entry mentioned in footnote 47. I am most grateful to Dr. Nicholas Vincent for helpful comments on the contents, and particularly for generously supplying the superior text of Appendix, no. 6. Above all I am indebted to Dr. O. J. Padel, without whose persistent encouragement this essay probably would never have materialised, and whose advice has often helped me, not least in the production of the text printed in Appendix no. 7—though imperfections which may yet remain are entirely my own handiwork.

12

THE PATRON SAINTS OF POUNDSTOCK AND HELLAND CHURCHES

Devon and Cornwall Notes and Queries, 23 (1947-9), 342-3

THOUGH THE ANCIENT DEDICATIONS of most of Cornwall's churches have been discovered or verified by modern research in medieval records there are still a few instances in which either no dedication is known or else the one that is known is of late occurrence, suspect, and unsupported by satisfactory evidence. Such an instance is the parish church of Poundstock. It is said to be dedicated to St Neot; but the assertion has never been justified. C. G. Henderson, in his notes in *The Cornish Church Guide*, challenged this dedication to St Neot, saying that he could find no authority for it, and that it probably rested upon a mistake. Again, in *The Cornish Church Kalendar*, he gives St Neot's Church as the only known dedication in Cornwall to that saint: Poundstock Church is pointedly omitted.

Recently, however, I was fortunate enough to discover that the missing patron of the ancient parish church of Poundstock is St Winwaloe, a very famous Celtic saint. In A.D. 1322 Bishop Stapeldon instituted to the rectory of Poundstock a certain Thomas de Knolle, who remained rector there until he exchanged benefices in A.D. 1348. The episcopal registers call his church simply Poundstock. In A.D. 1333, by good fortune for us, he was engaged in a County Court lawsuit, in the record of which he is described as Thomas, parson of the Church of St Wynwola of Poundstock (*Thoma Persona ecclesie Sancti Wynwolai de Pountestoke*) (Public Record Office, SC2/161/74, membrane 8 in dorso).

This adds a most important fact to our knowledge of the influence and cult of St Winwaloe, to whom the churches of Gunwallo, Landewednack, Tremaine, and perhaps Towednack, and chapels in St Cleer and St German's parishes are dedicated. Canon Doble has examined St Winwaloe's legend and cult in *S. Winwaloe*, no. 4 of the Cornish Saints series.

Thirteen years ago, in the *Truro Diocesan Gazette*, November, 1936, I was able to publish a similar discovery, this time concerning the dedication of Helland Church. A summary of that article may be of some interest now. The only dedication till then suggested for Helland Church was one to St Helena. This is not supported by medieval records, and is thought to be a mere guess, inspired by the name Helland. Henderson writes of this church 'Dedication unknown'. However, it appears in a deed of A.D. 1443 (Exeter City Library, no. 31,931), which came to my notice many years ago, that a certain John Colyn of *Hellond* created a Trust for the purposes, *inter alia*, of founding an obit for himself, his father and mother, friends and benefactors, in the Church of St Seninan (*Sancti Seninani*, but see *infra*), yearly on the Monday after the feast of St Lucy the Virgin, with Placebo and Dirige and Masses, and of repairing the houses and closes of *Hellond*.

This does not specify that St Seninan's Church is Helland Church: but it is extremely probable that the church in which Colyn intended to found this family obit was the parish church of Helland, where he worshipped, of which he possessed the advowson, which lay within his estate of Helland manor (*alias* Helland Gifford, *alias* Over Helland), and to which the last two rectors had been presented, the one by his father, the other by his widowed mother.

We may, I think, be confident that he meant Helland Church. It is true that no 'Colyn' obit appears in fact to have been established there: or, if it was, it escaped the notice of the Chantry Commissioners at the Reformation. But neither is one known to have existed at any other Cornish church. So that proves nothing.

Henderson has pointed out that 'The only saint connected with the parish appears to have been St Sinny (i.e. Sinini or Sithney) whose name is preserved in the small tenement of "St Cinney's Parks" adjoining the Cardinham boundary. St Synnies Gate is named in the bounds of Cardinham, 1613.' The name of Helland's patron, then, seems to be merely another form of St Sinny, or Sithney (for whom see Doble's Cornish Saints no. 18, *SS. Sithney and Elwin*).

I believe that Seninan is the best reading of the name in the deed of A.D. 1443. Owing, however, to the calligraphy of the period, and to the careless use of contraction marks by the scribe who wrote the document, warning must be given that the second two syllables of the name can be read in other ways, of which Sennian is perhaps the most feasible. In any case the colloquial form seems to have been Sinny, just as it was at Sithney Church.

13
ST GERMAN OF CORNWALL'S DAY

Devon & Cornwall Notes and Queries, 27 (1956-8), 103-7

IN THE SOUTH-EASTERN CORNER of Cornwall the two Cornish churches under St German's patronage lie within eight miles of one another. The little church of Rame parish stands high on its great promontory beside Plymouth Sound, while the once conventual church of St German's parish, venerable in Cornish history, is beautifully situated beneath the hill to whose feet the tidal waters of the St German's river formerly flowed. With the possible exception of a vanished medieval chapel at Padstow[1] no other Cornish church claimed St German as its patron saint: in Devonshire only the church of Germansweek appears to do so.

Ever since the 14th century the saint of these two Cornish churches has been identified with St German of Auxerre, whose day is 31 July, and whose burial is commemorated on 1 October. But it was not always so: the confusion of an obscure and dimly remembered local Celtic saint with this celebrated and similarly (if not identically) named bishop of Auxerre can be observed in a surviving record from Saxon Cornwall. From the Mass of St German (*Missa Propria Germani Episcopi*),[2] a liturgical fragment of the mid-10th century originally used at St German's, and from the *Pontificale Lanaletense*[3] of the 11th century, we learn that the Cornish name of the place afterwards called St German's was *Lannaled*, or *Lanalet*.[4] Moreover, the first of these two documents

---

[1] C. G. Henderson says it had a dedication to the two pre-eminent monastic saints of Cornwall, St Petroc and St German (G. H. Doble, *St German of Auxerre*, Cornish Saints series, no. 6 [2nd edn., 1928], p. 12, footnote: but in the later *Cornish Church Kalendar*, C.S. series, no. 31 [1933], p. 39, Henderson omits this dedication to St German).

[2] Bodley MS. 572, printed in Haddan and Stubbs, *Councils*, vol. I, p. 696; and also, with valuable notes, in *Pontificale Lanaletense*, Henry Bradshaw Society, vol. 74, p. xxi *et seq.*

[3] Bibliothèque de la ville de Rouen, A.27, Cat. 368, edited by G. H. Doble for the Henry Bradshaw Soc., vol. 74 (1937).

[4] The name predicates a Celtic monastery: a dispute about its situation has been decided conclusively in favour of St German's in Cornwall (see G. H. Doble's summary of the argument in *Pontificale Lanaletense*, Henry Bradshaw Soc., vol. 74, on p. x and its footnote 2, on p. xii, and on p. xiii, footnote 1).

shows that at the church of *Lannaled* the cult of a local saint was being ousted in the 10th century by that of St German of Auxerre. Thus the worshippers at *Lannaled* on St German's day heard in this Mass that he had been a luminary and pillar of Cornwall who had flourished at *Lannaled* and had been buried there—a natural enough description of a local Celtic saint, but one wholly irreconcilable with the known history of St German of Auxerre.[5] Yet in the same Mass they heard also unmistakable allusions to the latter saint's legend.[6] Here, as Dr. W. H. Frere points out in his preface to C. G. Henderson's booklet,[7] we can detect the church in a process of transition from its old patron to its new patron.

That process had been completed by the 14th century. In 1340 the neighbouring burgesses of Saltash undertook to pay yearly to St German's priory one pound of pure wax on the chief feast of St German 'which befalls close before the feast called Blessed Peter's Chains' (*solvendum in principali festo Sancti Germani quod accedit prope et ante festum beati Petri quod dicitur ad vincula*):[8] the day before the feast of St Peter's Chains is 31 July, St German of Auxerre's day. Again, in 1358 Sir Nicholas Tamworth brought back to this church from Auxerre some relics of that St German;[9] and three years later Bishop Grandisson issued an indulgence to the faithful who should visit these relics at St German's priory church on 31 July and 1 October and during the octaves of both feasts.[10] Thenceforth the patronal festival at St German's was the feast of St German of Auxerre, 31 July.

The inevitable consequence of this substitution of one patron for another was the elimination of those features of the older cult that conflicted with the newer, especially, of course, the older patronal festival as such. It is therefore of particular interest to find certain traces at both these churches of St German of something that looks remarkably like an earlier patronal festival on a different day from the one finally established at them.

---

[5] St German of Auxerre is not known to have visited Cornwall, and certainly had no time during his two visits to Britain to qualify in any sense as a Cornish resident. His body was never brought to this island.

[6] e.g. his dealings with Vortigern.

[7] C. G. Henderson, *Records of the Church and Priory of St Germans in Cornwall* (King's Stone Press, 1929), p. vii.

[8] G. Oliver, *Monasticon Dioecesis Exoniensis*, p. 5.

[9] *Register of John de Grandisson*, ed. F. C. Hingeston-Randolph, p. 1226.

[10] *Ibid.*

St German of Cornwall's Day

In 1284 the prior of St German's claimed, and a jury vindicated, before the King's justices at Launceston his ancient right (granted, as he asserted, by King Athelstan) to hold a yearly fair in his manor of St German's on the vigil and feast of St German.[11] At the Cornish assize of 1302 the prior again claimed and was allowed the same privilege,[12] and in 1343 the prior took the precaution of obtaining letters patent exemplifying the Chancery record of this last judgement of court.[13] In none of these three records is the date of this feast of St German expressed (in the last two the *name* of the feast is not mentioned either), but it is clear that it could not have been 31 July because in 1311, right in the middle of these proceedings, the Bishop of Exeter, who owned half the village of St German's but had hitherto claimed no fair in it, received a royal grant of an annual fair there on Lammas day, its eve, and morrow—31 July, 1 August and 2 August.[14] And these two fairs, the priory's and the bishop's, co-existed at St German's village continuously until the 19th century.

The muniments of the priory are lost, but the date, or approximate date, of its fair can be discovered from the post-reformation records of the priory's estate. This had long been known as the manor of *Lanrak*, or Landrake, and when the King's minister accounted at Michaelmas, 1539, for the revenues of the dissolved priory's manor of *Lanrak* he included an item of 8s. 7½d. from the profits of the manor fair.[15] In the troubled days of the next century this fair seems to have dwindled almost to nothing, so that a rental of Landrake manor made in November, 1652 says 'There was A Fayre kept yeerely within the Towne of St Germans upon the Last Thursday in Maye and as Longe as this Fayre was keept and accostomed the Towne of St Germans did pay xx^d yeerely to the Lord of the Manno^r of Landrake for the profitts of the Fayre as belonginge, but since the discontinuance and Decay of the Fayre the [*sic*] haue Refused to pay the same'.[16] One can hardly blame them. Nevertheless the fair was revived, possibly soon after the Restoration, but at all events some time before the death in 1702 of Daniel Eliot, Esqr.; for in 1712 the trustees of his Will granted to Robert Pitt, a helier of the town, a lease of the profits arising

---

[11] PRO, Just.1/111, m. 36d.
[12] PRO, Just.1/117, m. 63d.
[13] *Calendar of Patent Rolls*, Edward III, vol. 6, p. 110.
[14] *Calendar of Charter Rolls*, vol. 3, p. 183.
[15] PRO, Ministers' Accounts (Special Collections 6), Henry VIII, no. 454, m. 9.
[16] Cornwall County Record Office, Earl of Mount Edgecumbe's MSS., MTD 38/2.

from the stalls and standings of two yearly fairs in the borough of St German's, *viz*. the May fair, and the other on 1 August, called *Lamass Fair*.[17] Daniel Eliot not only owned the site and demesnes of the former priory but was also lessee of the episcopal manor at St German's, the manor of Cuddenbeak, and of some or all of the manor of Landrake[18] (for the past century separated from the demesnes); hence his, and his trustees', power to dispose of the stallage of the fairs of both manors. After this the May fair, mainly for the sale of cattle, appears in books of reference as an annual event on 28 May, e.g. in the years 1769,[19] 1792,[20] 1814,[21] 1823, [22] 1864,[23] 1878,[24] and 1910.[25] Soon after this its date was changed to the last Monday in May, continuing so for the next quarter-century. The present custom is to hold it on the nearest convenient day to 28 May.

An interesting account of the May fair as it was kept about the year 1820 was published in 1864.[26] It was held on two successive days, 28 and 29 May: the first day was devoted to cattle sales, though there were also stalls selling confectionery, while the second day was marked by the election of a mock-mayor of the borough, and festivities of a mixed May-day and Oak-apple-day kind. Although some of these revels may have been of comparatively recent introduction the two-day duration of the fair recalls the similar practice in 1284.

Thus this fair which, in the 13th and 14th centuries, was held by ancient custom on the vigil and feast of some St German, is found from the 16th to

[17] Royal Institution of Cornwall, Truro, C. G. Henderson MSS, Calendar no. 24 (Documents at Port Eliot), p. 147.

[18] The *ownership* of this manor (as of other estates of Sir Henry Killigrew who died in 1646) became the subject of protracted litigation between heirs, purchasers and mortgagees, lasting on and off for half a century, until Sir John Maynard's daughter, the Countess of Suffolk, established her right to it.

[19] *A Description of England and Wales* (Anon., 10 vols., 1769-70), vol. 2, p. 150.

[20] *First Report of the Royal Commission on market rights and tolls*, etc. (London, 1889-90), cited by G. C. Boase, *Collectanea Cornubiensia*, col. 1586.

[21] D. and S. Lysons, *Magna Britannia*, vol. 3 (Cornwall), p. xl.

[22] [F. W. L. Stockdale] *Excursions through the County of Cornwall*, part 4 (1823), p. 120; subsequently reprinted in various book-forms.

[23] *The West Briton and Cornwall Advertiser* [newspaper], issue of 6 May, 1864, p. 5.

[24] G. C. Boase, *op.cit.* [see note 20], col. 1589.

[25] Kelly's *Directory of Cornwall*, 1910, p. 124.

[26] *The West Briton and Cornwall Advertiser*, issue of 19 August, 1864, p. 6, 'The St Germans Nut Tree', contributed by Robert Blight (see Boase and Courtney, *Bibliotheca Cornubiensis*, p. 1076), who was born at St German's in 1804, went to school there, and left the town in 1822.

the 20th century being held in the last week of May, and during much of those last centuries it was held specifically on 28 May, which is none other than the feast of St German of Paris. The close connection between medieval fairs and the patronal festivals of their parish churches is too well known to need amplification here: it looks as if 28 May, or if not that then another day in the last week of May, was once observed at St German's priory as a festival of a quasi-patronal character, to which the most ancient fair in the parish was attached: a festival, too, of such vitality that its fair withstood throughout the centuries the otherwise triumphant onslaught of the cult of St German of Auxerre.

This conclusion raises another problem: whoever the original resident saint of *Lannaled* may have been he certainly was not St German of Paris—a personage who fits that 10th-century description of the patron even less than St German of Auxerre does.[27] How then did the May fair come at any time to be held on his day, 28 May?

It must be remembered that there is no clear evidence connecting the fair with that day until the 18th century, though it is no doubt very likely that this practice followed a genuinely ancient tradition. But all that is certain is that the fair, from the time of its emergence into view after the Middle Ages, has always been held in the last week of May; and there seems to be no reason to doubt that this persistent custom was also that of the Middle Ages themselves, going directly back to the fairs reported in those 13th- and 14th-century records already reviewed. It follows that the ancient feast of St German, mentioned in 1284, was in the last week of May; and it also follows that, this being so, its confusion with the well-known and misleadingly named feast of St German (of Paris) on 28 May was almost inevitable once its original patron saint had been forgotten. Just when this confusion established the fair on the feast of St German of Paris we cannot yet say: some more information about the fair in the Middle Ages is required before the point can be decided.

From a 15th-century manuscript of Tavistock Abbey[28] comes confirmation of this conclusion that the feast of the local St German must have been in the last week of May, and therefore close to that of St German of Paris. That abbey had property in Rame parish where, it will be remembered, the parish

---

[27] St German of Paris did not come to Britain at all.
[28] *The White Book of Tavistock Abbey*, Duke of Bedford's MSS. at Woburn Abbey, Table 4, A.3. I owe my knowledge of this to Mr. H. P. R. Finberg.

church was also under St German's patronage. The document recites the substance of a deed made on 19 July, 1309, whereby Gilbert, Rector [of Rame], recognised his obligation to render a certain sum of money each year to the abbot by two payments, one at 6 October, and the other 'at the feast of St German which is the last day of May'.[29] Here is independent evidence that as late as 1309 a feast of St German on the third day after the regular feast of St German of Paris was certainly known, and even singled out, at the neighbouring church that shared the priory church's dedication.

The traditions of the comparatively isolated church of Rame are likely to have changed rather more conservatively than those of the monastic, and formerly cathedral, church of St German's; so it is quite possible that we have here the uncorrupted tradition of the district, and that 31 May is the authentic festival of that Cornish St German who lived and died at *Lannaled*.

[A subsequent article by the Right Reverend Richard Rutt, bishop of St Germans, 'Missa Propria Germani Episcopi and the eponym of St Germans', *Journal of the Royal Institution of Cornwall*, n. s., 7 (1973-7), 305-9, discusses the liturgical passages and concludes that 'St Germanus of Auxerre is the only man certainly known to have been honoured as the titular saint of our church'; see also P. L. Hull, in a review of C. R. John, *The Saints of Cornwall* (1981), in *Devon and Cornwall Notes and Queries*, 35 (1982-6), 196-7. The author's comment on this (July 1998) was as follows.

> To my surprise some readers have supposed the second paragraph [of the above essay] to imply that references in the *Missa Propria* to acts of St German of Auxerre did not allude to him. Of course they did; though that leaves unexplained the ambiguous passage. This article only collects historical evidence, of varying pertinence, to show a kind of dichotomy existing for a long time at St Germans in Cornwall between products of scriptoria and those of local and rustic traditions. An explanation is offered; but certainty is not claimed.

The 'ambiguous passage' is that which claims, in the *Missa Propria*, both that the saint is St German of Auxerre, and also either that he is buried at the Cornish church, or that relics of him are preserved there. O.J.P.]

---

[29] This is a quotation from an English translation of the *White Book* (see note 28) found and kindly communicated to me by Mr. Finberg. He subsequently discovered the *White Book* itself at Woburn Abbey and verified the accuracy of this passage, collating it with the original Latin text on folio xxix b.

14

CALLINGTON AND KELLIWIC

Devon & Cornwall Notes and Queries, 27 (1956-8), 225-7

BEFORE EVER Geoffrey of Monmouth in the 12th century mentioned Tintagel Welsh traditions or romances had placed King Arthur's residence, the court to which he retired in the intervals between his exploits, at 'Kelliwic in Cornwall'. It occurs, for instance, in the romance of *Kulhwch and Olwen*, composed, according to Joseph Loth, at least as early as the end of the 11th century.[1] *Celliwic*, a parallel Cornish form with the same meaning of 'wood, forest',[2] is not now known as a Cornish place-name; but the general opinion of scholars, endorsed by Professor E. Ekwall,[3] has been that it is represented by the first element of the name Callington. From this theory Loth and C. G. Henderson have been the only notable dissenters.

Recorded forms of the name Callington (of comparable antiquity with the Welsh texts mentioning *Kelliwic*) do not, however, appear to support this derivation but show a simple development from an 11th-century and persisting form *Calwe-ton*, through a 12th- and 13th-century variant *Calwin-ton*, to *Calyng-ton* in the 14th century (with one known earlier occurrence). These early forms are *Calwetone*[4] and *Caluuitona* 1086,[5] *Calwinton* 1187,[6] *Calewiton* 1194, 1195, 1196,[7] *Calwinton* 1198,[8] *Caluinton* 1199 to 1212,[9] *Calwitun* and *Callington* 1220,[10] *Calweton*

---

[1] J. Loth, *Les Mabinogion* (Paris, 1913), pp. 27, 28.
[2] See R. M. Nance, *Cornish-English Dictionary* (St Ives, 1938), p. 87; also E. Ekwall, *Concise Oxford Dictionary of English Place-names*, 3rd edn., p. 79, 'Callington'. Ekwall allows an alternative derivation [of *Kelliwic*, O.J.P.] from *celli* 'grove' and *gwic* 'village', and J. Loth prefers this (J. Loth, *Contributions a l'Étude des Romans de la Table Ronde* [Paris, 1912], p. 64).
[3] E. Ekwall, *ibid.*
[4] The Record Commissioners, *Domesday Book seu Liber Censualis*, vol. I, fol. 120ᵛ (The Exchequer Domesday Book).
[5] The Record Commissioners, *op. cit.*, vol. IV, p. 94 (The Exeter Domesday Book).
[6] Pipe Roll Soc., vol. 87 (Great Roll of the Pipe).
[7] P.R. Soc., n. s., vols. 4, 5, 6.
[8] P.R. Soc., n. s., vol. 9.
[9] P.R. Soc. (Pipe rolls of these years in divers volumes).
[10] T. D. Hardy, *Rotuli Litterarum Clausarum*, vol. I.

1267,[11] 1284,[12] *Kallynton* 1330,[13] and *Calyngton* 1365.[14] Concurrent with some of these were the names *Calwylande* 1284,[15] *Kalwelond* 1285,[16] *Kallilonde* 1301,[17] and *Calilond* 1327,[18] by which were distinguished the lands and manor surrounding Callington, especially after that town had become partially independent of the manor in the 13th century. This large manor, thenceforth called Callyland, incorporated the present parishes of Southill and Callington and was in fact the Domesday Book manor of *Calwetone*. (In much the same way the Domesday Book manor of *Lanscauetona* eventually became known as the manor of Launcestonland, and [the Cornish] *Middeltona* as Middelland.) These early forms of *Callington* show that *calwe* or *calwi* remained in occasional use as the first element of the name from 1086 until 1284: by comparison with this consistent usage the other spellings have the appearance of secondary developments.

The attempts to identify Callington with a place, not necessarily Arthurian, called *Celliwic* seem to have sprung from an 11th-century mistranscription. Dunstan's letter of *c*.980-8 speaks of a Cornish episcopal estate as *Cællwic*,[19] and the same estate is mentioned again in the *Leofric Missal* about fifty years later as *Cælling*,[20] which looks speciously like *Calling*-ton. The evidence, however, has shown that *calwe* or *calwi*, not *calling*, was the early form of this element of Callington's name. Without the support of an identification with *Callington* the name *Cælling* can be associated with no place except the slightly earlier *Cællwic*, to which it avowedly refers. A mistranscription of *Cælluig* (for *Cællwig*) as *Cælling* by the author of this memorandum in the *Leofric Missal* seems to be the most probable explanation of his spelling of this name. It must be emphasised that unless the names themselves provide some evidence,

---

[11] *Calendar of Charter Rolls*, vol. II.
[12] PRO, Assize Roll Just.1/111, m. 36d.
[13] *Calendar of Inquisitions post Mortem*, vol. VII (proof of age of Nicholas Ferers).
[14] *The Register of Edward the Black Prince*, II, p. 199.
[15] PRO, Assize Roll, *loc. cit.*
[16] Devon and Cornwall Record Soc., *Cornwall Feet of Fines*, vol. I, no. 415.
[17] *Cal. of Inq. p. Mortem*, vol. IV (Edmund Earl of Cornwall).
[18] Devon and Cornwall Record Soc., *op cit.*, no. 676.
[19] A. S. Napier and W. H. Stevenson, *The Crawford Collection of Early Charters*, no. 7.
[20] A. W. Haddan and W. Stubbs, *Councils and Ecclesiastical Documents*, vol. I (quoting Bodley MS. 579, fol. 2).

there is nothing in history to connect Callington with *Cællwic* or with any other episcopal estate, much less with King Arthur's *Kelliwic*. It should be observed, too, that in *Celliwic* the stress is on the second element *wic*, in the Cornish way; whereas in *Callington* the stress is on the first syllable, in the English way. A point worth noticing is the absence at Callington of any major British fort such as Castle Dore, an Iron-Age earthwork re-occupied in the fifth and sixth centuries,[21] above Lantyne where the Cornish romance of *Tristran and Iseult* placed King Mark's residence.[22] If the Welsh references to King Arthur's court at *Kelliwic in Cornwall* are founded on fact a similar citadel ought to be in evidence in its vicinity, wherever that may be. Castlewitch near Callington is much too small, and Cadson Bury, some distance away, opposes rather than defends the Callington area.

I believe that the true explanation of the name Callington has nothing to do with the name *Celliwic*, nor with King Arthur, but is to be found in the proximity of Hingston Down, or more particularly its highest point, Kit Hill.[23] These, especially the spectacular hill, are the outstanding natural features of the district. Kit Hill is visible, a striking landmark, for a score of miles in almost all directions. The surrounding country was once well wooded, as its place-names prove, but the hill and down are too high and bleak for trees now, and the mention of *Hengestesdun*[24] (Hingston Down) in 838[25] shows that they were downland then. It was, surely, this great bare hill rising above its attendant woods that gave the name *Calwe-ton*, 'bare hill *tun*', to the *tun* whose lands lay at its foot and were called *Kalwelond*, or Callyland.[26]

On the name *Calwe* let Professor Ekwall speak. In his *Concise Oxford Dictionary of English Place-names* he writes of Callow in Herefordshire '[*Calua* 1180, ... *Calowe* 1292, ...] ... An O[ld] E[nglish] *Calwe* or *Calwa*, derived from

---

[21] Royal Institution of Cornwall, *Journal*, n. s., vol. I, Appendix (1951) ('Report on Excavations at Castle Dore').

[22] This romance was composed in Cornwall—see J. Loth, *Contributions*, p. 60 *et seq*.

[23] Kite Hill, now Kit Hill, seems to be a late name, perhaps less than 200 years old: the hill was formerly included under the name Hingston Down.

[24] Sir Frank Stenton, *Anglo-Saxon England* (Oxford, 1943), p. 745 (quoting the Anglo-Saxon Chronicle).

[25] Dated 835 in the MSS., the Anglo-Saxon Chronicle being three years short in its reckoning at this point.

[26] Callyland manor included part of Kit Hill and Hingston Down.

calu "bald, bare" and meaning "bare hill".[27] Of Caludon in Warwickshire he writes '[*Canledon* 1265, ... *Caludon* 1275, ... *Calwedon* 1292, ...] "Bare hill" ...'[28] And, lastly, of Callaughton in Shropshire, '[*Calweton* 1251, ... *Caleweton* 1284, ...] The first e[lement] is a derivative of CALU "bare", either a p[ersonal] n[ame] *Calwa* "bald man" or more likely a hill-name *Calwe* (or *Calwa*) "bare hill".'[29]

It will have been observed that the form *Calweton* cited here is also the earliest known form of Callington, and the evidence reviewed has demonstrated that *calwe* continued to be used as a first element of this place-name during the first 200 years on record. The name *Calwe-ton* exactly fitted Callington in the days when it was still the capital of *Kalwe-lond,* before its isolating change into a medieval borough.[30]

[The identification of *Kelli wic* is further discussed by O. J. Padel and P. Moreton, in Henrietta Miles and others, 'Excavations at Killibury hillfort, Egloshayle 1975-6', *Cornish Archaeology*, 16 (1977), 89-121 (at pp. 115-19). Later commentators have agreed that the etymology suggested above for Callington removes the possibility of either the Arthurian *Kelli wic* or the Saxon episcopal manor of *Cællwic* or *Cællincg* being located there. Furthermore, there is no need for the Arthurian *Kelli wic* and the Anglo-Saxon manor of *Cællincg* to have been the same place: identifying one does not necessarily help in identifying the other. On *Kelli wic* see further O. J. Padel, 'Some south-western sites with Arthurian connections', in *The Arthur of the Welsh*, edited by Rachel Bromwich and others (Cardiff, 1991), pp. 229-48 (at pp. 234-8). Ian Maxwell, 'The identification and location of Cællincg', *Journal of the Royal Institution of Cornwall*, [3rd series], 3, i (1998), 39-47, suggests that the bishop's manor of *Cællincg* or *Cællwic* is to be identified with the later episcopal manor of Tregear, in Gerrans parish, but acknowledges that place-name and archaeological evidence fails to support the identification. O.J.P.]

---

[27] E. Ekwall, *op. cit.*, p. 79.
[28] *Ibid.*
[29] *Ibid.*, p. 78.
[30] The change of the English *calwe* to *cali* or *cally* in Callyland and Callington raises suspicions that the name Kellybray, on the flanks of Kit Hill, has been involved in a confusion of this word *cally* with the Cornish word *celli*, 'grove'. *Kellybray* and *Kellybron*, hill-side names, are found here in 1337.

15
The Feudality of Pendrim Manor

When Reginald, earl of Cornwall, died in 1175 his surviving legitimate children were three daughters — Sarra, who had married Aldemar, viscount of Limoges, Matilda, who had married Robert, count of Meulan, and Dionisia, who married Richard de Redvers, sometime earl of Devonshire.[1] Surviving records indicate that their father must have given them marriage portions of lands in Cornwall. Thus Sarra must have received the large part afterwards known as the manor of Tywarnhayle Tyes of the great manor of Tywarnhayle in the parishes of St Agnes and Perranzabuloe; while Matilda must have had the two manors of Moresk and Rillaton, respectively in the parishes of St Clement and Linkinhorne. There are references to these tenures among the Public Records, but only two of them need be cited here. Thus in 1226 we find King Henry III ordering the sheriff of Cornwall to deliver to Aymand (*Aymarus*), brother of the count of Limoges, the land of *Tywardnail* which had belonged to Sarra his mother, to hold the same during the king's pleasure.[2] Similarly we find William, earl of the Isle (*de Insula*), fining with the king in 1204 to have, *inter alia*, the manors of *Moreis* and *Ridleston* which were the heritage of the countess of Meulan, which she gave to the same earl.[3] He was a brother of her husband, Richard de Redvers, whose sons he had succeeded as earl of Devonshire; so this transaction no doubt reflects some family arrangements between continental and insular relatives during this divorcing period. But no record known to the present writer declares what marriage portion her father gave to Dionisia: it has to be inferred, if possible, from incidental territorial and feudal records of Devon and Cornwall. The leading circumstance which emerges

---

[1] [I have not been able to consult W. L. Sheppard, on the daughters of Earl Reginald, in *American Genealogist*, 29 (1953), 13-17, referred to in *The Complete Peerage*, vol. XIV, *Addenda and Corrigenda*, edited by P. W. Hammond (Stroud, 1998), p. 207; the article was apparently unknown to Picken too. O.J.P.]

[2] *Rotuli Litterarum Clausarum*, edited by T. D. Hardy, 2 vols (London, 1833-44), II, 145a.

[3] *Rotuli de Oblatis et Finibus*, edited by T. D. Hardy (London, 1835), p. 235.

from such records is that, early in the 13th century and thereafter during the Middle Ages, the manor of Pendrim in the Cornish parish of St Martin by Looe was the only manor in the county which earls of Devonshire (first Redvers then Courtenay) held of the king in chief. They came to hold other Cornish manors; but those they held of mesne lords, not of the king in chief. In parenthesis it may be remarked that the distinction between tenure of the king in chief and tenure of the king as of his Cornish capital honour of Launceston Castle (at such times as the earldom or dukedom of Cornwall was in the king's hand) sometimes escaped escheators, whose inquisitions are occasionally confused about it.[4]

The singularity of this tenancy in chief of Pendrim by the earls of Devonshire becomes apparent when we reflect that, according to feudal theory as it had developed by the 14th century, there were only four classes of tenants in Cornwall who held of the king in chief. Ignoring, for present purposes, some irregular but transitory feudal dealings in Cornwall by King John,[5] we find these four classes were the following ones.

First, there was the earl or duke of Cornwall, when one existed. His demesnes and knight's fees far exceeded those of any other tenant. In the year 1166 his knight's fees had been reckoned at 215 and one-third of a fee.[6]

Second, there was the earl of Gloucester, within whose great honour of Gloucester were included certain Cornish manors which had been royal demesne in 1086.[7] They had subsequently been granted to Robert, earl of Gloucester (died 1147). These Cornish lands became subinfeudated, with their fees annexed to the Devonshire honour of Umberleigh, except the fee of the manor of Kilkhampton which became attached to the Devonshire honour of

---

[4] The creation of the Duchy of Cornwall in 1337 perpetuated the territorial arrangements of the former earldom.

[5] The most flagrant irregularity recorded was King John's intrusion in 1203 of an additional tenant, William Briwere, over the head of the existing tenant of the honour of Middellond [Milton, in Morwenstow parish, O.J.P.], part of the earldom of Cornwall then in the king's hand: see *Rotuli Chartarum*, edited by T. D. Hardy (London, 1837), p. 110a. [Compare *Rotuli Litterarum Clausarum*, I, 297b, and *Bracton's Note Book*, edited by F. W. Maitland, 3 vols. (London, 1887), II, 304 (no. 367). O.J.P.]

[6] *The Red Book of the Exchequer*, edited by Hubert Hall, 3 vols (London, 1896), I, 262.

[7] *Chilchetone, Conarditone, Gudiford, Bennartone, Melledham* and *Carewrge* (Kilkhampton, Connerton, Codford Farleigh alias Coswarth, Binnerton, *Melledham* a lost place-name in Trevalga parish, and Carworgie): *Domesday Book* (general editor John Morris), 10, *Cornwall*, edited by C. and F. Thorn (Chichester, 1979), 1.5 and 1.14-1.18.

Winkleigh. Both these Devonshire honours, however, were members of the honour of Gloucester.

Third, there were the ecclesiastical landlords who held their estates of the king either by knight's service or in frankalmoign.

And fourth, there was the earl of Devonshire who held the fee of this solitary Cornish manor of Pendrim as a member of his Devonshire honour of Plympton castle, itself held in chief of the king.

The earls and dukes of Cornwall reckoned their Cornish fees in fees Mortain; but these other tenants in chief reckoned theirs in 'great fees' of Gloucester.[8]

It is the contention of this article that Pendrim manor, which had been royal demesne in 1086,[9] was almost certainly transferred to Devonshire feudality when Earl Reginald gave it as the marriage portion of Dionisia to Richard, afterwards earl of Devonshire. Twelve Cornish manors which had been royal demesne in 1086 are afterwards found among the fees or demesnes of the earldom of Cornwall: Pendrim, on this view, would have been a 13th had it not been thus alienated.[10] It is difficult to account for the oddity of Pendrim's annexation to the Devonshire comital honour of Plympton castle by any other hypothesis.

In the 13th century the tenant of the manor of Pendrim held it, quite in a normal feudal fashion, of a mesne lord of its fee, who in his turn held its fee of another mesne lord, who (it seems) held its fee of the lord of Plympton castle. In earliest records it would not always be easy to determine which of these tenures was the one in point unless the reader had some knowledge of the families which held each. Consequently the following analyses will usually commence in the 14th century, when explicit records become more available, and will work backwards towards the sometimes cryptic notices of the 13th century. The reader will thus be better able to assess the latter.

---

[8] [On the large fees of Gloucester, and the smaller fees Mortain (five-eighths the size), see O. J. Reichel, "'Fees of the bishop of Exeter" in "Testa de Nevil"', *Transactions of the Devonshire Association*, 34 (1902), 566-74 (p. 570); O. J. Reichel, 'Feudal baronage', in *Victoria History of the County of Devonshire*, I (1906), 551-72 (pp. 570 and n. 4); and for the relative sizes, *Inquisitions and Assessments relating to Feudal Aids*, 6 vols (London, 1899-1920), I, 385. O.J.P.]

[9] [*Domesday Book, Cornwall*, edited by Thorn, 1.7. O.J.P.]

[10] [I find this statement difficult to comprehend and cannot name the 12 manors: see the note at the end. O.J.P.]

1. Tenure in chief

In the 14th century the Courtenays, earls of Devonshire, held the fee of half a knight in the manor of Pendrim as of their honour of Plympton castle. This tenure is explicitly stated in records of the years 1377, 1337 and 1310.[11] Similarly in the inquisition taken in 1263 after the death of Baldwin de Insula (earl of Devonshire) Pendrim (*Pendrine*) is said to be half of one knight's fee.[12] These statements show that its assessment at one knight's fee in the Pipe Roll of 1199 (discussed below) is demonstrably an error. The earliest reference to this tenure of Pendrim by an earl of Devonshire appears in the Pipe Roll of 1201, when Earl William de Vernun is reported to have paid one mark for scutage for half a knight's fee in Pendrim.[13] This, incidentally, represented scutage on half a knight's fee of Gloucester (like the rest of the fees of Plympton), not on half a fee of Mortain (like the Cornish comital fees).

2. Mesne tenure (1)

During this period the fee of Pendrim manor was held of the honour of Plympton castle by a family named Ferrers (*de Ferrariis*) which held estates on both sides of the River Tamar in Devon and Cornwall. In 1377 Martin de Ferrers held half a knight's fee in *Pendryn, Hiskyn, Polmorkyn, Landiore, Loo, Lothek* and *Clys* at the death of Hugh de Courtenay, earl of Devonshire, as of his honour of Plympton castle.[14]

At the inquisition held on 24 January 1337, after the death of William de Ferrers late in 1336, it was found that he died seised, *inter alia*, of half a knight's fee in Pendrim which he held of Hugh de Courtenaye, earl of Devonshire, as of the honour of Plympton. This William also held many other fees in Cornwall; but all of them, except Pendrim, were held of the Cornish honour of Trematon castle.[15]

In 1310 surveys were made of the knight's fees attached to the honours of Okehampton castle and Plympton castle, held at that time by Hugh de Courtenay before he became earl of Devonshire. A copy of these surveys was compiled

---

[11] See below, notes 14-16.
[12] *Calendar of Inquisitions Post Mortem*, I, 176 (no. 564).
[13] Pipe Roll of 3 John (1201), Pipe Roll Society, n. s. 14, p. 191.
[14] *Calendar of Inquisitions Post Mortem*, XIV, 319 (no. 325).
[15] *Calendar of Inquisitions Post Mortem*, VIII, 21 (no. 45).

late in the 15th century. Among the Plympton fees is an entry whose translation runs 'In the county of Cornwall there is half a fee which is called Pendrym which William de Ferrers (*Ferrariis*) holds there.'[16] This William was different from the one mentioned above.

Taking a long leap backwards from 1310, we come next to a Ferrers entry in the Pipe Roll of 1198. In it is recorded the debt owed to the Crown by Roger *de Ferrariis* for having [a writ of] right of half a knight's fee in *Pendrim* against Reginald Russel.[17] It is unfortunate that we do not know why Reginald was claiming this fee (of which a Roger Russel is soon to be found as the tenant of this manor, if indeed he was not so already). But at least this Pipe Roll entry, obscure though it is, shows that the Ferrers family had their interest in Pendrim before the end of the 12th century. In this connection occurs the demonstrable error, previously referred to; for when in the following year the clerk of the Pipe Roll of 1199 came to enter the payment of this debt owed by Roger de Ferrers, he carelessly omitted from the Latin sentence the little abbreviated word *dim.* and wrote *de feodo*, 'from a fee', instead of the 1198 version *de dim. feodo*, 'from half a fee', thus turning the half into the whole.[18]

3. Mesne tenure (2)

Another mesne fee of half a knight in Pendrim was held by the Cornish family called Dauney (*de Alneto*), whose residence was at the manor of Sheviock, not far from Pendrim and very close to the manor of (West) Newton Ferrers in Cornwall. In section 4 of this article it will be seen that the Dauneys were the immediate mesne lords of the actual tenants of the manor of Pendrim early in the 13th century and probably even before that. But the present writer has not succeeded in finding evidence showing of whom the Dauneys themselves held their half a knight's fee in Pendrim. The time-scale of the various tenures which we are considering strongly suggests that the Dauneys held it of the Ferrers, as also does the total absence of any indication that another family's tenure intervened between them. As to the time-scale, it seems that 60 years can scarcely have elapsed between about the year 1200, when the Dauneys' tenure is known to exist, and the earlier date when Reginald,

---

[16] Royal Institution of Cornwall, Truro, MS. HF/19/37, fol. 7v. (at end of Plympton fees); compare Henderson Calendar no. 17, p. 85.
[17] Pipe Roll of 10 Richard I (1198), Pipe Roll Society, n. s. 9, p. 173.
[18] Pipe Roll of 1 John (1199), Pipe Roll Society, n. s. 10, p. 184.

earl of Cornwall from 1140 to 1175, must have held Pendrim manor in demesne, before bestowing it upon Richard de Redvers with Dionisia in marriage. Yet into that 60 years must somehow be compressed no less than four subinfeudations of the manor and fee of Pendrim. Firstly, there was the grant of the manor to the earl of Devonshire; secondly, there was the grant of the manor by an earl of Devonshire to a Ferrers (or an ancestor); thirdly, there was a grant of the manor to Dauney; and fourthly, there was a grant of the manor to its actual occupants—Russel or Bodrugan or an unknown ancestor of one or other of them. (Their tenure will be discussed in the next section.) It is clearly improbable that a fifth subinfeudation, involving some persons mysteriously absent from all surviving records, ought to be hypothesised between the Ferrers and Dauney in this already sufficiently crowded 60 years of feudal development.

John Dauney died in 1346 holding, among his various fees, one knight's fee in *Trehauek* and *Pendrym*; it is not stated of whom he held it.[19] This is Trehawke in the parish of Menheniot, next Sheviock, and it was held ultimately, through mesne lords, of the honour of Trematon castle in Cornwall, at this date a member of the Duchy of Cornwall; whereas Pendrim, as we have seen, was held of the Devonshire honour of Plympton. So, whatever administrative reason there may have been for uniting Trehawke and Pendrim in a single knight's fee in this record, the two places cannot originally have been feudally united. In a list of the knight's fees of the former Dauneys' manor of Sheviock, which was compiled (according to its internal evidence) between 1377 and 1394, a certain Richard Sergeaux is shown to be holding a life estate in one knight's fee in *Pendrym*: presumably the fee of Trehawke is implicitly included with this, for Trehawke is not mentioned in this list.[20] Richard Sergeaux, it may be remarked, was tenant of Pendrim through marriage with the heiress of Sir William de Bodrugan, sometime lord of Pendrim manor.[21] Some other

---

[19] *Calendar of Inquisitions Post Mortem*, VIII, 475 (no. 648); the first name is printed as *Trehanek*.

[20] Antony House, Cornwall, MS. PG/B2/9.

[21] Many Bodrugan estates, including Pendrim, descended to Elizabeth, first wife of Sir Richard Sergeaux, as daughter and heiress of Sir William Bodrugan, under an entail made by her grandfather, Oto Bodrugan, in 1387: *Cornwall Feet of Fines*, edited by Joseph Hambley Rowe, 2 vols (Exeter, 1914-50), II, no. 759. As Richard Sergeaux retained Elizabeth's estates until his death in despite of the entailed rights of Sir William's younger brothers, it would seem that Elizabeth must have borne him a living child, though it is unrecorded, thereby enabling her husband to retain possession of her lands 'by courtesy of England'.

records attribute half a knight's fee to Trehawke. For example, in 1402-3 Warin Ercedekne (lord of Penpoll manor in Quethiock parish) died seised, *inter alia*, of half a knight's fee in *Trehauk, Polpry* and *Bromene*.[22] Again, in 1285 half a knight's fee in *Trehauek* formed part of the dower of Joan, relict of the lord of Halton manor in St Dominick parish.[23] These records strengthen the supposition that the one knight's fee, mentioned above, in *Trehauek* and *Pendrym*, of which John Dauney died seised in 1346, comprised two separate fees of half a knight each, one of which referred to Pendrim. More references to the Dauneys' mesne lordship of the fee of Pendrim will appear in the next section of this article, where evidence of the family's early association with this tenure will be given.

After the death of Sir John Dauney in 1346 his lands and fees were carried by his daughter and sole heiress in marriage to Sir Edward de Courtenay. When their son and heir, another Edward, inherited the earldom of Devonshire with its honour of Plympton castle he found himself, as lord of Sheviock manor, owing the service of half a knight's fee in Pendrim to, probably, one of the heirs of Ferrers, who owed the same service to Edward himself, as lord of Plympton—a circular kind of service.

4. Manorial tenure of Pendrim

In 1331 Sir Otto de Bodrugan died overseas at Montpelier. He had been implicated in the earl of Lancaster's rebellion, but had recovered his lands.[24] Perhaps it was to insure his estates during that turbulent episode that he settled them unusually. At all events the inquisitions taken after his death and the death of Henry, his son and heir (who died before he knew of his father's death or had seisin of his lands), show Pendrim manor, which Sir Otto had with the borough of *Loo*, now East Looe, and the advowson of the church of St Martin as being held in parcels of Nicholas Dauney (of his manor of Sheviock, though that is not stated) and not as a single tenement of half a knight's fee.[25] But an earlier inquisition made in January 1309, after the death

[22] *The Hylle Cartulary*, edited by R. W. Dunning, Somerset Record Society, 68 (1968), no. 230 (printed as *Trehank*).
[23] *Ibid.*, no. 225 (printed as *Trehanek*, and wrongly identified as Trehannick).
[24] PRO Lists and Indexes, no. v, *Ministers' Accounts* (vol. I), p. 450, n. 9 (bundle 1,146, no. 21).
[25] *Calendar of Inquisitions Post Mortem*, VII, 276 and 278 (nos. 385-6).

of Otto's father, Sir Henry de Bodrugan, records that he held Pendrim, with the borough and the advowson, of Sir Nicholas Dauney as of his manor of *Shevyok* by service of half a knight's fee.[26]

The first of the name Bodrugan known to have held Pendrim manor in demesne as of fee was another Sir Henry de Bodrugan, great-grandfather of the above Sir Henry and a man of considerable consequence in Cornwall.[27] He inherited Pendrim from his mother, Lucy Russel, who in her widowhood styled herself 'lady of Pendrim'.[28] Her husband, Roger Russel, similarly described himself 'lord of Pendrim', but it is likely that he did so in his wife's right.[29] It is not known if Henry de Bodrugan was Lucy's son by an earlier husband. This Roger Russel was perhaps an official in the service of King Richard or King John;[30] but almost nothing is really known about him. Even his surname may have been a sobriquet.

What is certain is that Lucy Russel in her widowhood paid 12 marks to Bernard Dauney (*de Alneto*), son of Henry Dauney, to ensure that Bernard would receive the homage of her son, Henry de Bodrugan, for Pendrim, without further payment of a relief upon his succession to the tenure. The text of Bernard's receipt for this fine, reciting these particulars, has been preserved; it may perhaps be assigned to the period between 1210 and 1225.[31] The fact that Bernard, issuing this receipt, styles himself the son of Henry strongly suggests (a) that his father had been mesne lord of Pendrim before Bernard was, and (b) that Bernard had recently succeeded his father. This Henry Dauney was alive in *c*.1180 and 1201.[32]

There remains one document which, if it were complete, would obviously throw light upon the obscure complexities of the tenures of Pendrim at the

---

[26] *Calendar of Inquisitions Post Mortem*, V, 65 (no. 139).
[27] See chapter 10 of this volume.
[28] *Ibid.*
[29] *The Cartulary of Launceston Priory*, edited by P. L. Hull, Devon and Cornwall Record Society, n. s. 30 (1987), no. 464.
[30] The Bodrugan Cartulary (section *Tregrehon*) records a grant made to him by William Hay 'at the king's command' (*precepto Regis*): Royal Institution of Cornwall, Henderson Calendar no. 26, p. 89; the cartulary itself is Cornwall Record Office, Truro, MS. ME/595.
[31] *Ibid.*, p. 111 (section *Pendrim*).
[32] H. P. R. Finberg, 'Some early Tavistock charters', *English Historical Review*, 62 (1947), 352-77, at pp. 363-4 (no. XXIX), and n. 12 for the date; *Pleas before the King or his Justices 1198-1202*, vol. II, *Rolls or Fragments of Rolls from the Years 1198, 1201 and 1202*, edited by D. M. Stenton, Selden Society, 68 (1949), p. 34 (no. 138).

beginning of the 13th century. Unfortunately a vital surname in it has been destroyed, so that its full import cannot be determined. It is a final concord made in the year 1201 by which, upon a plea of *mort d'ancestor*, three daughters of William Baucan, Sibilla, Juliana, and Margaret, quitclaimed their right in four-fifths of half a knight's fee in *Pendrin* to the tenant in the action, Roger [.....], who for this quitclaim gave Sibilla and Juliana five silver marks, and to Margaret half a mark.[33] It so happens that at about this date the tenant of the manor of Pendrim, Roger Russel, and the tenant of its mesne fee, Roger de Ferrers, shared the same christian name; either of them might be meant here. In the present writer's opinion this concord about portions of half a knight's fee in Pendrim is likely to represent dealings with the Ferrers' mesne lordship. The Ferrers family must have had dealings with the Devonshire family of Baucan because by the year 1336 half a knight's fee in Norton Baucein in Devonshire belonged to William de Ferrers, who also held the half fee of Pendrim.[34] This, of course, is a mere straw of evidence, though it may have the proverbial use of a straw.[35]

Addendum

[Note on the statement made above, 'Twelve Cornish manors which had been royal demesne in 1086 are afterwards found among the fees or demesnes of the earldom of Cornwall: Pendrim, on this view, would have been a 13th had it not been thus alienated.' (p. 127). It is hard to understand this statement. In Domesday Book King William held 17 manors in demesne (or, in the Exeter text, he himself held 12 manors and Queen Matilda five) (*Domesday Book*, ed. Thorn, 1.1-12 and 1.14-18). Of these 17, six were given to the earl of Gloucester (as shown above, n. 7). This leaves only 11 manors (including Pendrim), not thirteen. Of these, three manors are found later as demesne of the earldom of Cornwall (Helston in Kerrier, Towan or Tewington, and Climsom or Climsland: *Domesday Book*, 1.2, 1.3 and 1.9); a further five manors, at least, were held in fee of the earldom (or, later, of the duchy of Cornwall):

---

[33] *Cornwall Feet of Fines*, I, no. 15.
[34] Inquisition post mortem of William de Ferrers; see note 15, above. [The half-fee in Norton Baucein was stated to be held of John de Doune. O.J.P.]
[35] [Presumably for making bricks of substance; compare *Exodus*, chapter 5. O.J.P.]

Winnianton (*DB*, 1.1),[36] Lanow (St Kew) (*DB*, 1.4),[37] Blisland (*DB*, 1.6),[38] Penheale (*DB*, 1.12),[39] and Callington (*DB*, 1.10).[40] It may be that the remaining two demesne manors apart from Pendrim (Caradon [?] and Roseworthy, *DB*, 1.8 and 1.11) were also so held, and may be found by diligent searching in the records, such as inquisitions post mortem. Many other manors which had not been royal demesne in 1086 were also part of the later earldom and duchy, either as demesne or held in fee. But even if all the manors held in demesne in 1086 (except for Pendrim) were so held, it is unclear how any total greater than 10 could be arrived at. O.J.P.]

---

[36] Inquisition post mortem of Sir John Arundell, 1435: PRO, C.139/72, no. 39.
[37] *The Caption of Seisin of the Duchy of Cornwall*, edited by P. L. Hull, Devon and Cornwall Record Society, n. s. 17 (1971), p. 9.
[38] Duchy of Cornwall accounts, 1447-8, Cornwall Record Office, AR2/719, m. 9.
[39] *Caption of Seisin*, p. 8.
[40] *Caption of Seisin*, p. 125.

PUBLICATIONS OF W. M. M. PICKEN

* = reprinted in this volume.

Old Cornwall
'The Domesday Book and east Cornwall', 2 (1931-6), xi (Summer 1936), 24-7.
'Caradon Lyer in the parish of Linkinhorne', 3 (1937-42), 59-63.
'Landiok', 4 (1943-51), 418-23.
'The place-names of Morval', 5 (1951-61), 131-3, 143-9 and 186-97.

Devon and Cornwall Notes and Queries
'East Looe Corporation MSS., Part I. Two rentals', 21 (1940-1), 129-30.
   [Supplement to C. K. Croft Andrew, 'East Looe Corporation MSS, Part I. Two rentals', 21 (1940-1), 88-96.]
'Charaton and Penhawger', 23 (1947-9), 202-5.
*'The patron saints of Poundstock and Helland churches', 23 (1947-9), 342-3.
'The Cornish heritage of the Bonvilles, by descent from Champernoun and Fitz Walter', 24 (1950-1), 227-30.
   [Supplement to J. Benson, 'Alice—Fitz-Roger, Bonville, Carminow, Rodney', 24 (1950-1), 56-8.]
*'Trezance, Lahays and the manor of Cardinham', 26 (1954-5), 203-8.
*'St German of Cornwall's day', 27 (1956-8), 103-7.
*'Callington and Kelliwic', 27 (1956-8), 225-7.
'The meaning of Barton', 28 (1959-61), 23-5.
   [Supplement to W. G. Hoskins, 'The meaning of Barton', 23 (1947-9), 273-7.]
'The descent of Coode of Morval from Prouz, Moeles and Daumarle', 29 (1962-4), 142-5.
   [See also addendum by H. M. Peskett, 'The Coode family of Morval', 32 (1971-3), 22-3.]
'A Tonkin MS. in the British Museum', 29 (1962-4), 281-2.
*'The names of the Hundreds of Cornwall', 30 (1965-7), 36-40.
*'Light on Lammana', 35 (1982-6), 281-6.
*'Tremail and Turgoil in Domesday Book', 36 (1987-91), 269-73.
'The Beville Obituary II', 36 (1987-91), 354-62, and 37 (1992-6), 35-41.
   [Supplement to C. Henderson, 'The Beville Obituary', 16 (1930-1), 17-26.]
'Stumwoedgan in Cornwall', 37 (1992-6), 173-5.

'The genesis of two Cornish place-names in the thirteenth century', forthcoming (2000).

Journal of the Royal Institution of Cornwall
*'The manor of Tremaruustel and the Honour of St Keus', n. s., 7 (1973-7), 220-30.
*'The earliest borough charter of East Looe', n. s., 8 (1978-81), 350-7.

Cornish Studies
'Saint Laud in Cornwall', 8 (1980), 48-52.
*'A misdated Cornish tax account in the Book of Fees', 10 (1982), 19-25.
*'Cornish place-names and fiefs in a twelfth-century charter', 13 (1985), 55-61.
*'Bishop Wulfsige Comoere: an unrecognised tenth-century gloss in the Bodmin Gospels', 14 (1986), 34-8.

The Cornish Times
'Caradon Lyer, in Linkinhorne parish', 7 January 1938.
    [Substantially the same as the article in *Old Cornwall*.]
'Re-naming Seaton', 28 April 1950.
'Lost tenements of St Martin', 11 November 1955.
'Barcelona' [in Pelynt parish], letters, 24 February, 30 March and 4 May 1956.
    [In response to articles on 10 and 17 February; compare other letters on 24 February, 2 and 16 March, 20 April and 11 May.]
'Trevabyn: the story of a search', 15 March 1957.

Other places
*'The "Landochou" charter', in W. G. Hoskins, *The Westward Expansion of Wessex* (Leicester, 1960), 36-44.
'A Spanish battleship's bell in Cornwall', Royal Institution of Cornwall, *Newsletter*, 13 (April 1993), 4.